A COGNITIVE PROJECT

Steven Blackwell

Kindle Direct Publishing

https://kdp.amazon.com

Copyright © 2021 by Steven Blackwell

All rights reserved. No part of this book (or copies) may be used, reproduced or transmitted in any form or by any means whatsoever. This includes, but is not limited to, electronic or mechanical, photocopying, recording or transferring to any storage or retrieval platform; without exclusive permission from the publisher or the author.

Published in Canada, by Steven Blackwell

ISBN: 9798718136647

Steven.blackwell1010@gmail.com

This book is a work of non-fiction. All content is based on a researched opinion from the author and contributors and is not based on scientific or professional knowledge.

Production Credits

Foreword by Matthew Broughton

Edited by Sandra Blackwell and Grammarly Premium

Cover Creation by Steven Blackwell in Canva

Head Shot: Jennifer George Photography

Written, Designed, Published and Printed in Canada-2021

A
COGNITIVE
PROJECT

Also, by Steven Blackwell

232 Birch: A memoir of the haunted house we used to live in while residing in a home on Vancouver Island. Ghosts do exist…232 Birch confirmed it.

The Pale Murphys: A fictional novel about a young family who moves into a haunted location. A horrible fire kills the previous owners in a great tragedy, and one of the spirits wants revenge, not quite ready to rest yet.

Jakob Sterling: The thrilling fictional novel and sequel to The Pale Murphys. The Sterling family has to face a possession from one of their own, and it would appear as if the spirit of Jimmy Murphy still haunts them.

Mister Tom: An implausible fictional novel about a series of outlandish coincidences that bring two separate groups together while a young girl meets a new friend who she hopes to free from the deserted Fijian island.

Cascadia: A truly gifted ten-year-old girl speaks to her deceased mother, and they predict the most devastating earthquake ever to hit. Can she save her father in time?

Coming Soon

A Second Cognitive Project

Featuring: The Moon Landings, Nuclear War, Aliens, Ghost Stories, Atlantis, Natural Disasters and much more!

A Cognitive Project

Dedication

I am highly honoured to dedicate this, my sixth book, to a beautiful friend and cherished member of my extended family.

Grace Pelletier

Thank you for your continued support and loving memories over the years.

A Cognitive Project

Foreword

By Matthew Broughton

To conspire...*make secret plans jointly to commit an unlawful or harmful act.*

Can we legitimately say the words, "they conspired against them," and it is factual, without modern-day fact-checkers combing through every piece of the internet to either validate or debunk said unlawful or harmful act?

Let's rewind a little, back a way, a long time ago. According to the Holy Bible (both versions) and other accounts, the Romans conspired to murder Jesus Christ, the supposed son of God, born to a virgin, where three wise men came from afar to bring gifts for the child for his birth. This miracle child was unique. He did all sorts of exciting and pretty much illogical things that wowed the small-minded population back in those times. So, the Romans conspired to murder Jesus. Then, once Jesus was nailed to the cross, he died on Good Friday and was resurrected Easter Sunday. Come on. Really?

I believe that religion is a form of population control, just like modern-day media, which has captured a captive audience's attention. However, only you can be the judge of your own sacred beliefs and opinions.

The simple fact that around the world, there are several locations that are quite sacred to indigenous populations, which are some of the wonders of the ancient world. Could those locations have served as landing spots for travellers from other worlds? Who is to say that the theory of the ancient gods is right or wrong? Sumerians were a very advanced civilization, based on some of the archeological finds and writings.

Speaking of writings – if there's something people could not explain, wouldn't they write it off to "the gods?" Were these simple people the true indigenous earthlings? Were those mighty gods merely interstellar travellers, and are we not ultimately their descendants? Or were we given some of their DNA to manifest our own very own evolution?

You will hear in this book about various conspiracies and ideas, which will provoke introspect about your own beliefs, including facts. Yes, facts. Have they been checked? Are they legit? Who oversees said fact-checking? Are they reputable and honest?

Did we really land on the moon? Or was it filmed, as the band, Red Hot Chili Peppers wrote in their hit song "Californication" – made in a Hollywood basement?

I once spent some time in Dallas, Texas, and drove the Grassy Knoll route where JFK was assassinated.

A Cognitive Project

Were there two shooters? Was it a CIA assassination? Was Lee Harvey Oswald the killer, or just the fall guy?

How do two giant structures, made of steel, collapse from two planes striking them? The simple fact that the twin towers' collapse looks like a controlled detonation should spark a significant number of questions.

Everyone remembers where they were, during the moon landing, the JFK assassination and on 9/11. I am not specifically into conspiracy theories. I am into wake the fuck up; it is so damn apparent, theories.

However, I am always open to new information on the subjects in this book. The author and I have had extensive conversations over the twenty-five years we have been friends about these subjects. The what-ifs, the why, the how, the where, when, and primarily who.

The current COVID crisis provokes some food for thought. Yes, the disease is real. Yes, it kills (although I'm sure you will find the author's family's own experience with COVID interesting), and yes, it is sad. The food for thought is what was happening prior to this scourge? Worldwide, there were populous uprisings in democratic and non-democratic nations. The Hong Kong democracy protests were hitting a breaking point, where you know that Mr. Jinping wanted to send in the soldiers and take them out. That's what Chinese communists do.

The media followed, Yellow Vest protests, the rail blockades in Canada over some significant pipeline expansions and integral resource development. Once the worldwide pandemic was declared and the world was thrust into lockdown, suddenly, these people went away. Hong Kong is now as close to undemocratic as can be.

What better way to take back control over the masses than a pandemic that kills less than one percent of those it infects? Now don't get me wrong, I am all for taking precautions, and I haven't had more than a few sniffles in nearly two years. But we are all allowing it to happen. Now that it has happened, the government will not forget how easy it is to take back control of the population.

This leads me to the cancel culture. Cancelling out past events. Who is behind this? What is their end goal? I am confident the readers have their own opinions on this, and in my mind, it is simply societal conditioning.

Censorship. The social media giants shut down what they feel is inappropriate, sites like Parler, as they foster a different way of thinking? How long before the thought police take complete control and the only voices of dissent or differing thoughts will be whispers in the night, in alleys and the corner of taverns. Can you trust your neighbour? Is this the modern-day conspiracy that George Orwell foretold in his famous book, 1984?

A Cognitive Project

Simply take away the right to speak about what you think, and not only are we into censorship but also walking a dangerous line towards an Orwellian future.

No one can tell the future - however, history always tends to repeat itself somehow, in some shape or form, in more modern ways. I hope you, the readers, never have your voice silenced and, most importantly, never resort to giving up your friends and neighbours to the thought police if they refuse to be silenced. Most of all, if you do not like something you see on the internet and get offended? Keep scrolling on by, don't feel like you need to go through the process of reporting someone.

This may eclipse most of what I intended to speak of, and while I do not want to steal Steven's thunder, I think he will agree with me on the previous few paragraphs. I know we are well aligned in the first part of my opinion.

It is not the job of myself, nor the author of this book, to change your mind or beliefs. It is only to expand your horizons on some fascinating subjects. Closed minds, narrow-mindedness and tunnel vision are all keys to disaster. So, open your mind, open your eyes, and question everything. Please enjoy Steven Blackwell's latest book. I know I will!

- Matthew Broughton
March 2021

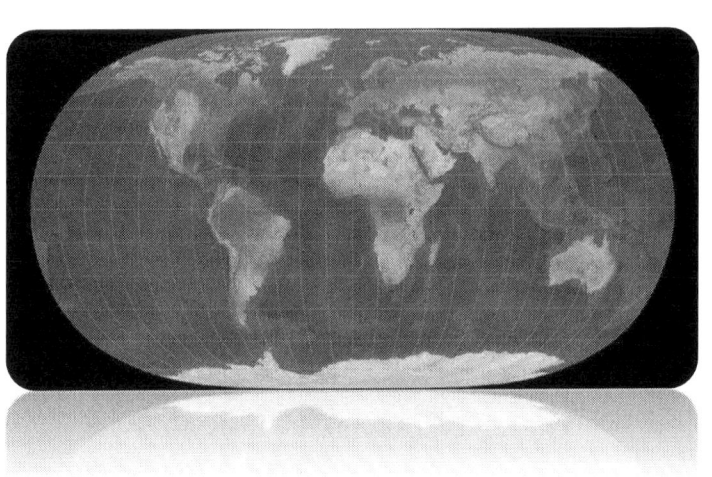

A Cognitive Project

Introduction

As I prepared to sit down and write this book, many different emotions passed through my mind. I realized that no matter how much research I did, I could never find the absolute correct answers. The opinions on most subjects are objective and can be contradicted by another person's simple hypothesis. I started by treading lightly.

I must confess that I do not wear a tinfoil hat, but much of what I'm writing about in this book could be classified as *conspiracy*. Keep in mind that a conspiracy theory is a simple way to debunk a story said to us by mainstream media in most cases and intelligently thought out to enlighten the subject differently. It contests the 'official report' and is usually greeted by skepticism and disdain from the general public as a rule. But why do we conform? Why are we afraid to speak up?

The numerous pundits related to these subjects have asked questions from day one, and the following opinions will be just that. An argument based on research and decision-making. This allows me to look closely at both sides and make a refined choice on my conclusions. Asking these questions will enable us to grow as a species and educate ourselves on the facts. Not just what we've been told, but the honest and believable facts.

I certainly don't expect to change anyone's mind or shift their faith. I can appreciate the opinions that others have, so this will be mine, and I'll stress that I don't hold any expertise in these subjects. But I'll be the first to agree that we have all been lied to for many, many years. This will never change, but it's how we accept those lies that define our very intelligence as a species. We are brighter than we appear at times. Here's a look at all of the topics I'm going to discuss in this Cognitive Project.

The chapters in this book include my opinions on the *Paranormal*, which is close to my heart. I'll even discuss what scientists believe, and their conclusions may be pretty surprising to some of you. The paranormal is a vast subject, but although my experiences have been with the spiritual supernatural, I'll also touch on other anomalies, such as Aliens, Bigfoot, and the subtle Loch Ness Monster. Our existence is full of strange mysteries.

I'll also dive into the tragic events of *Nine-Eleven* and the strange anomalies from that day that goes entirely against the official report. From the 'planes' to the *collapse* of the three towers, including *Building 7*. I'll dissect the *Pentagon* incident, as well as the alleged *Flight 93* that supposedly crashed into an empty field in Shanksville, Pennsylvania. Whether you want to believe it or not, the events of nine-eleven may actually be the biggest cover-up in the history of modern times.

A Cognitive Project

We'll break down a bit of the controversy with an entertaining chapter about some fantastic *animal stories* that I've experienced in my life. I'll share eight short stories with you that are entirely true. I'll also include two stories that are *not* true. This will show us how easily we can be manipulated into believing *the mainstream media's actual story*. See if you're able to distinguish the true stories from the fictionalized events. These past events have burned into my mind as forever memories.

I've included a fascinating chapter on *Religion* and Christianity in particular. I've kept close track of my faith throughout the years. I've taken the time to do the research, allowing my gut to feel comfortable. The words I will share in this section are merely one person's non-professional opinion, but perhaps it will enable you to look at your *god* a little bit differently.

Our vast *Universe* will be another interesting topic to debate. The idea of dark space, time and distance seem to boggle many of us, but the probability of extra-terrestrial life in the universe seems almost certain and inevitable. This chapter will propose a few probable scenarios that lie in an entirely different evolutionary period. We'll explore distant planets orbiting around their shining stars and the most common opinions of our species' intelligence of aliens that may have been fooling us for our entire lives. We are unquestionably not alone.

We'll take a closer look at the John Fitzgerald *Kennedy Assassination* and try to make sense of where the fatal shot rang out. Was Lee Harvey Oswald responsible for the President's death? You may be surprised by what I have to say about this subject. An event that happened before I was born and this subject will continue to be debatable for many more years.

Also, the great *Ancient Pyramids* and *Megalithic Structures* around the world. We've been told specific timelines for the construction of these objects, but now scientists are gradually discovering that these impressive erections may have been built much earlier than first thought and reported. Reports that span from generation to generation, fooling the child who has no choice but to take their un-educated opinions into adulthood.

I'll offer quite a vague opinion of the mysteries behind *Quantum Physics*. I know very little about this kind of math, but it's always intrigued me. After researching on my own, it's evident that some brilliant men and women have taken science to a new level and uncovered parts of our current reality as a complete hoax. Do you think it's possible that we all may be living in a hologram? Has our validity ever really been confirmed?

And finally, a chapter on our very own Mother *Earth*. We'll take a look at a brief timeline of the planet's long

A Cognitive Project

existence, and try to understand *time* as it relates to our lives. There has been more than one catastrophic 'reset' on the planet. Ice ages and cosmic events have reshaped the resilient planet and offered life options for literary *billions* of years. Think of the numerous species that may have ruled the Earth back then. Any evidence of a species billions of years ago would have certainly faded.

Whether you agree with me or not, it's not essential. Respecting someone's opinion should be acceptable and allows us to see different perspectives. I may be way off with my thesis, but my words will be honest and from my heart. Looking at both sides is a much easier way to base a credible opinion, and I believe this book will allow you to broaden your minds on these subjects. The powers of the world are hiding quite a bit from us. The evidence is starting to pile up, and with human's determination, the truth is imminent, and opinions will be changed around the world. We only need to open our minds and secure our beliefs as accurate and true. Stand firm and take control of your destinies while you can. And enjoy your life as you know it. Our next life may not be as pleasant, but we will manage. We always seem to survive in the end. And that's because the end for one of us will always be the beginning for another. How we decide to live our short lives is up to each one of us as individuals. We will learn more, and life will still evolve.

"I understood at a very early age that in nature, I felt everything I should feel in church but never did. Walking in the woods, I felt in touch with the universe and with the spirit of the universe." – Alice Walker

A Cognitive Project

The Paranormal

The simple idea of 'The Paranormal' runs much deeper than many even understand. It's not just a bump in the night or the hairs on your arms standing at attention. Fear is a common emotion that exists within us all, but fear of the paranormal stems more from the unknown than the fear of a five-foot clown doll hiding under the bed with a sinister smile and a four-inch kitchen knife. That would be horror, and it's an entirely different kind of fear than *paranormal fear,* which is an unknown fear.

Paranormal is not horror. It simply means something that has not been scientifically explained yet. Not only are we getting closer to achieving closure on some anomalies that we have been steadfast to believe or *not believe* for many generations. I'll focus on the spiritual paranormal, but there is a lot out there that we still don't know or understand as human beings—much more than you can even believe. Our evolution has offered us great strides in technology and luxurious comfort, but we are still trying to wrap our heads around some everyday needs. Our mighty oceans, space, and humanity during and after death still boggle some scientists and leave a void of vital information. There are so many topics, and

I'll touch on a few of them, starting with the *Spiritual Paranormal*. It's an experience that I've witnessed firsthand and on more than one occasion at separate locations. No one can tell me ghosts don't exist.

When I first encountered the spiritual paranormal, I was a young boy growing up in Saskatchewan. It was what I witnessed, twenty-five years later, in *232 Birch* that made me do some more research on the supernatural and afterlife energies. I convinced myself that ghosts existed, and since then, I've realized that thousands of others have made the same claims. I began to accept the stories of others, realizing that I wasn't bat-shit crazy.

People started telling me stories of their loved ones standing at the end of their beds in the night and evident energy pressing down on their blankets. Or even some mysterious sounds, music or verbal communication. I collected this data and reached out to more people. I had knowledgeable and logical individuals tell me they've never told anyone else their stories before. They were afraid to be viewed as crazy or misleading, but I started to see a definite pattern after a while. These perfect strangers were telling me similar experiences, striking a chord with my own episodes, and building credibility on the subject. Certainly, we couldn't all be incorrect.

A Cognitive Project

I started closely looking at the numerous videos and photographs available online. From orbs to full-bodied apportions, I studied them all and tried to debunk each one. Some, I was able to find reasonable explanations, whether they were purely natural or apparent fakes, but some of the material still makes me shake my head.

The trouble was that no matter how credible I found the photograph or video, there were always skeptics who would be crystal clear that the material was tampered with and *faked*. This news frustrated me for a couple of reasons. First, I knew that there were fakes out there, many of them. Sometimes you can tell within the first few seconds of the viewing. Still, I found it hard to believe that the literal thousands and thousands of digital shreds of evidence existing of the spiritual paranormal had all been manipulated. I asked myself two simple questions. I know quite a bit about computers, *could I make that video look like that*? And if I could, *how long would it take me*? It just wouldn't entertain me to lie.

I began asking some of my friends if this would be a feat they could quickly achieve. All of them would admit an emphatic *no*. Then I asked them if their friends could do it, and again, after some thought, most of them admitted that it would be challenging and quite skillful to add these types of effects. Yes, it could probably be accomplished with today's photo and video technologies, but there are so many to discover. Some of the evidence is raw, CCTV video that has been shared with news agencies and paranormal enthusiasts, right out of the camera. And then there is some evidence that we can't deny. In my opinion, this energy exists all around us, as it awaits its new life, wherever that may be. I wondered what the scientists had to say, and it shed some light on the subject, which explained some of the claims.

To date, scientists believe the spiritual paranormal to fall into one of two categories. They are as follows.

Pareidolia

"*Pareidolia is the tendency for the incorrect perception of a stimulus as an object, pattern or meaning known to the observer, such as seeing shapes in clouds, seeing faces in inanimate objects or abstract patterns, or hearing hidden messages in music.*" -Wikipedia

Sleep Paralysis

"*Sleep Paralysis is a state, during waking up or falling asleep, in which a person is aware but unable to move or speak. During an episode, one may hallucinate (hear, feel, or see things that aren't there,) which often results *in fear. Episodes generally last less than a couple of minutes. It may occur as a single episode or be recurrent."* -Wikipedia

We also know, through science, that an *electronic magnetic field* can cause simple deficiencies in the brain, such as unbalance, paranoia, and at times, crippling fear. These magnetic fields are energy sources that emit from power, such as electrical outlets and running water. This energy is often apparent in water wheels or hydro plants.

These definitions can justify many experiences and creepy tales of the paranormal, and I'll admit that. But it doesn't explain the lot to me. These theories have a few holes. Sometimes the credibility from the storyteller of an experience can't be denied. It's genuine and holds validity. And some of these accounts just can't be debunked, no matter how hard you might try. Our brains may fool us sometimes, but we can recognize anomalies.

If multiple people witness the same anomaly and video evidence is tangible and correct, the theories above won't apply. Pareidolia makes perfect sense, but the truth is, if more than one person can validate a photo or video, it must mean that what they are seeing is indeed there. A face in a cloud or in an oak tree is one thing, but to see this energy in our everyday reality is quite different.

So now I can hear a haunted tale and debunk many of the claims. Science has taught us that so far. But the continual evidence that no one can explain is what I'll continue to focus on. It would appear to me that the many scientists and spiritual professionals that concentrate on this puzzle may still have some work to do if we are to fully understand this enigmatic realm. Appreciating this may very well solidify our soul's journey after our death and bring us some peace for a new beginning.

I'm a true advocate of reincarnation. It just makes sense to me. It would seem to be a natural transition from death to life and back to death again. The possibilities are endless, and they cry for an explanation, making me think everything is just a simple chemical reaction.

My belief about death is straightforward. We have a powerful body and a brain that we know very little about. I believe that the brain holds our soul or life's energy. Some may call this a spirit, and in my opinion, this is our ghost, and it stays close to us throughout our lives.

When our body dies, it becomes but a shell for our soul. Your brain will eventually die, and I believe our soul is then released into our reality. The soul may be confused, as it has lost its sacred and secure body. Even the cause of death itself could prevent your spirit from

A Cognitive Project

knowing that your body has stopped working. This may allow it to wander aimlessly as it tries to find a way to start again. It is during these times that the living can witness this spiritual energy. Sometimes this energy can haunt for hundreds of years. Still, there is uncanny evidence that some of this energy can find an immediate opportunity to begin anew, reincarnated into an original, fresh-born human body, and another faithful chance.

If this is the case, I believe that the soul would be an unintelligent irregularity. It may just cause a residual memory that plays like a tape recorder, over and over. I have also witnessed, what I would call, intelligent spirits. This still confuses me, suggesting that energy can communicate and physically manipulate objects and people. Either way, I would imagine that the emotions and feelings that we held in our brains would be lost. In short, it would make sense to me that if we can't remember our reality before we were born, we probably won't remember any kind of our reality after we've passed on. Just a deep blackness while the soul learns.

It may help us to understand Deja-Vu or perhaps even our dreams, as strange as they may be. Our souls may hold memories from past lives and allow the new body owner to reminisce about earlier times in history.

The Paranormal

Regardless of your sacred beliefs, skeptical or not, we can all agree that something exists that lacks explanation on the spiritual paranormal. I'm relatively optimistic that many of the scientists will continue to find evidence that may explain our lives, as well as our existence after our deaths. The discovery will be epic and ground-breaking.

For those who haven't read my first book, 232 Birch, here is a quick recap of my personal experiences. When we lived in the townhouse on Vancouver Island, my wife, children and I had about ten peculiar happenings.

We started hearing odd noises coming from within the walls at the bottom of our stairs. It was challenging to describe correctly, and it wasn't something easily recognized with today's knowledge. This bizarre sound was only heard one night, and then never again.

And then my wife and I saw a little boy outside in the pouring rain. He was translucent, and it was well after midnight. The boy stared at us and even raised his arm to the outside of our home. By the time I reached the main floor and opened our sliding glass door, he was gone. But he was there. For us, there was no doubt.

This same boy showed up a couple of years later, walking past my wife's peripheral vision and heading up the stairs to the second floor. She thought it must be our son, who had recently begun to walk. Our son was on the couch watching the TV. But she saw the boy again.

Our infant daughter was physically moved within her crib. This was after four years of strange occurrences in that nursery. At this point, we believed that we had at least two spirits living with us: a boy and an adult male.

When some of our possessions were moved around without our knowledge, we knew we weren't alone. We had an infant swing start up on its own and move by itself for a good three minutes as we stared in complete terror.

Our final experience at 232 Birch shaped my beliefs on the spiritual paranormal. As we said goodbye to visiting guests, my wife and friends all witnessed the anomaly of a prominent male figure's shadow passing by the door's window and heading upstairs where my children were sleeping. Of course, as per usual upon investigation, we were unable to see or capture proof of this man. But it all came together in the time we lived in 232 Birch. We concluded after we moved out that the spirits of a small boy and an adult male may have lost their lives in or around the townhouse. This energy was intense while living there, and the activity was peaceful and intriguing. Most definitely, 232 Birch taught us a valuable lesson.

In 2014, we took a vacation to Arizona. We made it a point to stop in world-famous Tombstone, which is full of ghostly tales, notably the Birdcage Theatre, coined as one of the most haunted sites in North America.

We could smell the history, and it felt as if we had been transformed into the old, wild west. There were spirits in the Birdcage Theatre. They were watching, and many would have sustained traumatic injury and death.

My wife and I took over two hundred photographs of the building, from the extravagant stage to the back stage area and the infamous poker room downstairs. And across from there, the rooms that could be rented. Upon further inspection of the pictures, we found at least three of them that contained anomalies that just couldn't be explained. I have included these photos in 232 Birch, but they clearly show some sort of manifestation. This energy is strong. It's persistent and remains around us.

We'll shift gears a bit and discuss another significant paranormal obstacle in our current reality. We've asked the questions for generations. *Do aliens exist? Are we alone in the universe? Have we already been visited by aliens?* These questions demand answers, and I think some of us know more answers than others. Is this another cover-up? It certainly seems to be possible.

A Cognitive Project

We know there are just as many videos and photos of UFOs as ghosts and spiritual energy. Some of these supposed captures have been faked or misinterpreted by the witnesses; that much is clear. We've been wired to think of Roswell, New Mexico, and Area 51 in Nevada as hot spots for extraterrestrial proof, but the contents of these venues are still subject to debate, and we must ask ourselves why. Secrets are being held from us for sure.

These places have been kept secret from the general public for many, many years. It's pretty clear to me that the American government knows a great deal on this subject, even to the point where they may very well be involved in talks with visitors from outer space.

Suppose we can conceive the enormous vastness of space and the perception of many light-years, molecular movement, and distances that are sometimes difficult to wrap our minds around. In that case, we must believe in some form of life elsewhere in the universe. We would be naïve to think it wasn't probable and silly to think it wasn't possible. In fact, the potential is truly endless.

Considering we are only one species on this planet, we have perceived the beginning of our lives on many different scales. Life, for us, was possible because of the *building blocks of life*. These elements occur because of our planet's proximity to our star, *The Sun*. The building blocks of life would include *Carbon*, *Oxygen*, *Hydrogen*, *Nitrogen and Phosphorus*. Without these five elements, human beings would not be able to exist. These would need to be accompanied by a planet that wasn't too hot or too cold for humans to survive comfortably. And the atmosphere that protects us and offers us life-required freshwater could be the most crucial of all. We take it for granted at times, but it's essential for our procreation.

It would make sense to me that if these elements are present on Earth, just one look at the clear night sky would suggest that they can exist in literally trillions of places. We only see a portion of our great cosmos, and from what we can already tell, all distant stars are sheltering orbiting planets. Some of them could easily be within the same proximity from their star as we are here on Earth. If that's the case, the building blocks of life may exist. When we consider the number of planetary objects that we know nothing about, the probability of some sort of life is almost certain. We only need a little bit more time and some extra patience to discover them.

We can then take the evolutionary phase of that living organism, and within millions of years, another world could easily support intelligent lifeforms. I'll admit that these lifeforms could be humanoid in concept, but the idea of many different-sized and shaped species would make just as much sense. Remember, we don't even know some of our animal species here on Earth.

Some of these species may have evolved over billions of years, and perhaps they have extracted a higher level of technology than we have already. There would be other planets that are in a different timeframe of their existence. These planets may support an early form of life that still has millions of years to catch up to us on Earth. They, too, may wonder about other life in space.

I believe the UFO footage captured worldwide, and much more common nowadays is a combination of different aircraft. They could be simple drones or some sort of experimental military aircraft. The government has kept this delicate information somewhat secretive, and these strange sights are unidentified by the average human who witness them. But I do believe that some of these aircraft are not from our world. Even NASA had started releasing odd anomalies in space, and they just can't be explained by anyone at this time.

So, if this sort of intelligence is out there somewhere, it could be a species that has evolved far past that of human beings. They would have the technology to travel through the cosmos, and a visit to our planet may be nothing more than curiosity. Most of the opinions on extra-terrestrial life will be adamant that the visitors are coming to destroy us. But perhaps this particular species isn't bloodthirsty like humans seem to be. Maybe they have no logical use for us. They may only view us as unintelligent, lost beings who have a tremendous amount to learn still. We must grasp that we may not be superior.

I mentioned earlier that it's even possible that these aliens may already be here. More and more evidence of shapeshifting and time travel suggests that these beings may indeed be visiting us and maybe even collecting research to assist their cause. Perhaps the United States government knows more than we've been told. There could be a very distinct possibility that more than one species is working together for reasons that remain a mystery to the rest of man and womankind.

Many other cases could be classified as 'paranormal.' Two folklore tales come to mind, and I've wondered what the truth was, as long as I can remember. The first would be the secrets of the Bigfoot or Sasquatch. Also called the Yeti or Abominable Snowman, the Bigfoot is considered a folk story. There are increasing reports, and again they seem to be supported by enchanting video and photo evidence that can't all be explained. I mentioned earlier that we don't know all of the species inhabiting our planet. Most of these creatures would be found in our undiscovered oceans, but it makes me wonder...is the elusive Bigfoot real? If they are, we need better signals.

Could there possibly be a species that is crossing the generational and evolutionary gap? Maybe a continual species that has adapted to wilderness life and learned how to avoid human beings at all costs at an early age. Sure, there are lots of fakes out there. It's become a pretty fascinating subject and has been reported on, like aliens, for plenty of years. We can assume these anomalies have probably been witnessed for thousands of years and never reported. The other option to bogus claims of the Bigfoot could be a species that once existed but doesn't anymore. A rolling stone gathers no moss, and stories like this can survive for generations. If this creature is out there, it will need to be captured or killed. This will stop all negativity and skepticism once and for all.

The same would be true about the second 'mythical' being that we've all grown up with. The infamous Loch Ness Monster has been an unidentified creature from Loch Ness's depths in Scotland's highlands. Nessie, as she's been affectionately called, has only been reported on since 1933. Most of the photographs and videos have been disputed, and cases are being closed as a hoax. There never seems to be enough clear evidence.

But like the Bigfoot, this creature may have existed many years before discovered by mainstream media. Witnessed by settlers from the beginning, and perhaps this serpent-like creature may have died off. Or it may live in the depths and remain shrouded from human beings, only being witnessed every once in a long while. This animal would most likely be some sort of eel or large fish, and that fact supports scientist's claims that almost every species studied by archeologists suggest that the animals were larger than today's ancestors. This goes for the human being as well. A Giant species is said to have existed. But that may have to be another project.

So, to sum things up on the paranormal. I try to think as realistically as I can on a subject. You'll notice that with the coming chapters as well. I try and look for the most common explanation before believing any kind of story. As mentioned, it should depend on who shares the information with you. Some people can be considered entirely trustworthy because you know them, and you know their unique personalities. But they could also be mistaken, or the scientific explanations of Pareidolia and

Sleep Paralysis could be a factor in these experiences. There could very well be one more factor in our brains to consider. Perhaps we control more than we know.

Our Pineal Gland

Most vertebrates on Earth have a pineal gland in their brains. This special gland produces melatonin, which is a serotonin-derived hormone. It helps to modulate our sleep patterns and could be linked to the paranormal. Our brains are a mystery. They allow us to feel pain, love, remorse, and empathy, among other quality traits. We feel all of our emotions through response from our brain, and it may very well be the window to our afterlife. The Pineal gland could possibly be giving our senses the wrong information depending on the scenario. Or maybe it connects us with our past lives and clarifies our reality. But until more study and understanding is concluded on the brain, we have to consider that the paranormal may be something this gland is trying to tell us. One thing is for sure. Medical experts have coined the pineal gland 'The Third Eye,' and many believe it to be *The Principal Seat of our Soul*. If we really think about it, our unknown brains possibly hold all the answers we've been looking for. We can't harness the power of our minds to the fullest extent, but imagine if that time was ever to come.

The Paranormal

For now, the world will be full of people who believe in the paranormal, as well as a significant number who think the entire topic is false. There isn't enough evidence to announce the phenomenon as fact or 'proof.' That day may very well come someday, though, as we grow more intelligent as a species. When that day comes, there will still be skeptics out there, and at the end of the day, we all have the right to trust what we want to for inner peace. Regardless, things will continue going bump in the night.

The reason the paranormal is so interesting is that we genuinely don't understand it. Most events tend to take place at night or in the dark. Scientists say that this would be why our brain tells us to be scared. It's because we have limited visibility, and our brains will make things up that may not actually be there. You're probably safe, and there's really nothing for you to worry about usually.

I hear stories from people who say they wake in the night and see a loved one standing in their bedroom corner. Or they are maybe sitting on the edge of their bed. Most people admit to closing their eyes or covering their heads under the bed covers, and when they look again, the misty apparition is gone. This has never personally happened to me, but I've had my own experiences and take these stories seriously. Maybe everything isn't truly a ghost, but until we understand what's happening to millions of people worldwide, we will call it paranormal and admit that a spiritual realm must exist somehow.

My advice is simple. The next time you see a door move on its own or hear a voice in the rafters. Rub your eyes, and make sure you're awake. When you smell the aroma of fresh cigar smoke in a building where smoking isn't allowed, shake your head, and pinch yourself. If you wake in the night and the hairs on your arms are standing straight up, you may see the energy of a loved one who has passed. Don't cover your face in fear. Say hello and try to communicate. Whether this is a mind trick or not, it brings us peace and hopes for tranquillity after death.

And remember that UFO and alien headlines are more prevalent than ever before. The evidence is becoming overwhelming, and if you think it's all doctored, I would have to disagree with you respectfully. We've been waiting long enough for answers. If Bigfoot, The Loch Ness Monster, Ghosts and Aliens are real, we're closer than ever to finding undeniable proof, and skeptics may very well become believers, right in front of your eyes.

The rest is up to you. Open your mind and consider the possibilities that remain our 'paranormal.' We just need more knowledge of our biggest fear, the unknown.

"The Twin Towers were brought down by a controlled ground explosion, not the planes. Now I tell you in passing that among the friends I have are consultants who work for the world's leading civil engineering and construction firm. I'm not going to name it, but they have studied the film for me. And they have said that there is absolutely no doubt whatsoever that the Twin Towers in New York were brought down by a controlled explosion." – Alan Hart/Journalist and Author

A Cognitive Project

Nine-Eleven

I can remember it like it happened only yesterday. It was a Tuesday morning, September eleventh, 2001. More than twenty years already, and some adults weren't even alive when it happened. But it happened, and it shook the world. For me, it was almost like watching a Hollywood movie. Once we're finished with this chapter, you may admit that it was more of a scripted tragedy than we thought. The sad truth, though, is that this movie was real and took thousands of innocent lives. Those victims' families demand the truth about that tragic day, as it seems evident that it didn't transpire precisely the way the mainstream media reported it to us, even days after.

Like many of you did, I turned on the news broadcast shortly after the first 'plane' hit the north tower. I was in shock and assumed there had been a horrible accident. It wasn't long before the journalists were reporting that a 'plane' had hit the tower. First, they reported that a small craft had made an impact. But before long, the infamous video (and the only one available) of the commercial airliner smashing through the side of the steel-enforced structure surfaced. Even before the second impact on building two, the entire world was convinced that an airplane flew into the World Trade Centre. Because that's what we were told, and that's what we could see. The story of Osama Bin Laden and his terrorist following solidified it for the people of the world. A foreign enemy had attacked the United States, and now they would have an excuse to purge the infidels and their already skeptical religious beliefs. Unfortunately, prejudice was involved.

We all think we saw the second 'plane's impact, but *truth be known*, we saw a video, recorded by media, of a large commercial airliner striking the building and appearing to go right through the structure itself. They started showing the travesty, over and over again, and after time, in many different angles and positions. I was certainly convinced. It was the most *honest* thing I'd ever witnessed in my life. People were dying, though, and it was only the first act of a strange and disturbing day.

We all watched as the buildings burned and the heroic firefighters made their courageous way forward while everyone else rushed back and away from the dangers. People started to jump to escape the suffocating smoke, a decision I couldn't even imagine having to make. And the media continued to affirm us of the terrorist attack.

Then, they reported on the Pentagon and another 'plane' that had been hijacked and flown into the side of the most secure building on the planet. I was shocked. *What was next*, I thought. Somehow, I had a feeling that the events of the day weren't finished yet. We were all confused, and rather than looking at the quick facts, we empathized with the deceased and quickly learned to scorn the announced enemy threatening the west.

I watched the buildings collapse in a pancake fashion. The devastation of the moment didn't allow me to realize that had never happened before, to any other structure, unless it was orchestrated by controlled demolition.

I needed to get away and left the house, but it didn't matter where I went. If there was a television, it was on. Then they reported on the fatal 'crash' near Shanksville, Pennsylvania, and when I saw the crash site's ariel footage, I raised my eyebrows on this event for the first time. In fact, I've probably researched the events of 9-11 more than any other subject, and there are far too many holes in the official story to ignore. Here's the official report, as told to everyone in the world. *This is 'what happened' and has been written in our textbooks.*

The following is an authentic excerpt from the official 9-11 Commissions Report. This is what most people think happened on that fateful summer day.

"Four passenger airliners departed from airports in the North Eastern United States bound for California *were hijacked by 19 Al-Qaeda terrorists.* Two of the planes, American Airlines Flight 11 and United Airlines Flight

175, *crashed into the North and South Towers, respectively, of the World Trade Centre complex in lower Manhattan*. Within an hour and forty-two minutes, *both 110-story towers collapsed*. Debris and the resulting fires caused a partial or complete collapse of all other buildings in the World Trade Centre complex, *including the 47-story 7 World Trade Centre Tower*, as well as significant damage to 10 other large surrounding structures. A third plane, American Airlines Flight 77, was *crashed into the Pentagon* (the headquarters of the U.S. Department of Defense) in Arlington County, Virginia, which led to a partial collapse of the building's west side. The fourth plane, United Airlines Flight 93, was initially flown toward Washington, D.C., but *crashed into a field near Shanksville, Pennsylvania,* after passengers tried to overtake the vile hijackers."

- Wikipedia

I've italicized the words or subjects that I will discuss further in this chapter. In this case, there is more than one smoking gun, and most of the scientific evidence can't be ignored. We'll look at the events as they unfolded, and I'll wrap up the nine-eleven chapter with my official but non-professional opinion on the most likely series of events that took place. Remember, if there seems to be a lack of evidence presented, we have to consider the possibility of cover-up or conspiracy in this case.

A Cognitive Project

Commercial Aircraft were used on four different occasions. Two into the twin towers, one into the Pentagon, and the other into a field in Pennsylvania.

When I first noticed people disputing commercial aircraft used, I looked into it very closely. I looked at both sides and weighed the numerous video evidence supporting both sides of the argument. Some claimed that no airplanes were used on 9-11. Others proposed some sort of experimental military weapon was used, and the plane was superimposed on top of it for the media to share with everyone watching. This would be the news video we saw, over and over again. After years of looking at the evidence I have at my disposal, I believe that it may have been a combination of these theories.

At first, I agreed with the 'Truthers.' I confessed that no planes were used, and the world had been fooled. This bothered me, though, and I had to dig deeper. If you search the second 'plane' colliding with the south tower, you will see multiple angles showing the airliner hitting the building. Surely, all of these couldn't have been tampered with. (Does this sound familiar from the paranormal chapter?) It's quite evident that something flew into the building. Still, eyewitnesses from that day reported hearing an explosion that occurred from inside the building, and they never saw or heard a plane before the ball of fire erupted from all four walls. *How could an airplane cause an explosion that resonates through the entire internal area of the impacted floors?*

So, maybe two aircraft did hit the towers, but were they commercialized as they reported? I must confess, I do love science. It makes the unbelievable credible and allows us to broaden our imaginations of what's to come. A few months, after 9-11, I started to ask myself how an airplane could penetrate a steel re-enforced structure and cause a fire so hot that the buildings would both fall in the exact same way. There would be some significant discrepancies with the 'planes,' and science can help prove that some of the reports from that day are false. If you believe nothing else about nine-eleven, please remember this because the physics don't make sense.

We have to look at the most prominent issue here. *Aluminum cannot fly through steel.* Yes, speed times velocity can be argued, but the speeds needed, no matter what we were told, were not enough to penetrate a columned steel building. The planes should have broken up upon impact and rained aircraft pieces on the streets below. The jets just wouldn't have been able to enter the structure, let alone cause an explosion that shook entire floors around the complete perimeter. This may be difficult to fathom, but let's theoretically look at the scenario in reverse. When I first read this, it was very logical, and science's reality just can't be unseen here.

A Cognitive Project

Imagine, if you will, a Boeing 767 suspended in midair. Now imagine a 110 story, steel re-enforced building flying through the air at 300 miles per hour. Ask yourself what happens to that airplane when the building makes contact with it. The aircraft won't pass through the building. As a matter of fact, the building will more than likely swat the plane out of the sky like a housefly, causing minimal external damage to the steel structure itself. This would physically work both ways, but what we witnessed repeatedly and what the news told us completely contradicts this science. So, what could have possibly compromised the steel-beamed construction?

You'll find out my opinion on this at the end of the chapter, and you may disagree, but if an object flew through the air and struck these buildings, it must have been something more than a commercial aircraft, and having an understanding of that may help us slowly piece together all of the events from September eleventh in a proper way. An optical illusion simply tricked our minds.

I should point out that the second aircraft's reported estimated speed when it hit the building was more than 500 miles per hour. Yes, an airliner can achieve those speeds, but there's a huge issue with these claims. Large commercial aircraft weren't designed to soar at high speeds while at low altitudes. Physically, it causes many problems that disrupt the very aerodynamics, and pinpoint accuracy wouldn't have been possible. Again, the objects that hit the towers may have been travelling at those speeds, but they just couldn't have been the commercial aircraft reported. The facts are missing here.

The Towers Collapsed in the same way because of steel beams melting from the airline fuel's heat.

When the buildings collapsed, it became so real to me. At that moment, thousands of innocent people lost their lives, and I just couldn't believe it even happened. Just like everybody else, I witnessed the one-hundred and ten-story structures collapsing, floor by floor, upon themselves like nothing I'd ever seen before. But then I thought. *Wait, I have noticed that before, more than once.* Only weeks after the horrific day, I was convinced that controlled explosives brought the buildings down. It was precisely the same way it was done on abandoned or weak buildings. This is an intricate process that takes time and cooperation to achieve correctly, but now I needed to research the living hell out of this anomaly.

As difficult as it was to believe the fantastic structures could just fall, it was the extensive research I did, after the fact, that made me highly question this most tragic event from that day. It was the incident that caused the most death. The following are points that I learned after the fact, and they question the tragic collapse story.

- An Israeli corporation that leased two floors of one of the towers severed their agreement and moved out of the Trade Centre only a few weeks before the incident.

- There were several reports of multiple floors closed to the general public while some maintenance procedures took place. These would be the opportunities to set the buildings up for a controlled demolition.

- There were steel beams found at ground zero that were clearly cut by machines at forty-five degrees. This is standard practice for any controlled explosion and is consistent with some eyewitness accounts admitting that men were using high-powered tools before the attack.

- The official report simply stated that the airliners' fuel burned so hot that it melted the steel beams, causing the buildings to collapse. Science has proven that the heat created from a jet's fuel cannot burn hot enough to melt steel to a state of sufficient failure and collapse.

- Recovery crews found 'channels' of molten steel running down the beams at ground zero. Truthers highly believe that this was caused by *Thermite*, an explosive used in most controlled demolitions. These molten pools ran throughout the site after the collapse and explained why the location burned underground for more than a week after the disaster. These pools of molten metal are inconsistent with many of the 'official' reports.

Nine-Eleven

- Multiple eye-witnesses on the streets below reported hearing explosives *popping* down the building as it was collapsing. Much of the collapses' video evidence clearly shows puffs of white smoke exploding from the buildings' corners, consistently just a few floors below the collapsing buildings' apex. Even explosions were heard from the lobby of the 110-story building. The only way to drop a building of this size is to have all of the steel columns blown out and failing in succession. Remember, no steel assembly has ever collapsed from fire, and buildings cannot pancake upon themselves without a highly coordinated effort by professionals.

I'll wrap up my thought and opinions of what I think caused the catastrophic collapse of World Trade Centre's one and two at the end of this chapter. It shouldn't have happened, and if we could re-create the scenario to scale by flying a remote Boeing 767 into a steel re-enforced building, I think we would all witness a whole different outcome. We would see a shattered aircraft at the base of the structure. There would be fire damage, and most of the windows in the impact area would have blown out. But the buildings would stand, and the many firefighters who risked their lives heading in while others were trying to get out could have possibly survived and gone home to their families that day. It was a feeble and sad, unnecessary plan that lacked a proper cover-up.

Building 7 – The Salomon Building

This building, too, encountered a cascading failure or progressive collapse. It wasn't even hit by a 'plane.' Those who claim a conspiracy theory have been accused of 'wild claims,' as it accepted worldwide raging fires, buckled the building and made it the pancake. I'm not disputing that uncontrollable blazes that burned all afternoon may have caused some sort of structural failure, but again, a skyscraper has only collapsed two other times this way in history. Unfortunately, it was only a few hours earlier when the Twin Towers fell. Thankfully, building 7 was vacant, but all was still lost.

Ironically, the Salomon building was the storage place for all of the United States' personal and secure records. Any documentation of what happened that day most likely would have burned in the fires, along with the truths. I'll give my opinion of the World Trade Centre at the end of the chapter, but after some research, something about building 7 stood out to me, and it fit my theory. This was part of the plan, and it fooled us again.

After watching numerous videoed interviews from that day, and the months following, I noticed and agreed with some very compelling evidence that involved the 'planes,' as well as the collapse of building 7. It was clear that some of the footage reported and shown by specific news networks was tampered with. CGI experts could see anomalies with some of the videos, and this evidence is available for anyone to search. What I learned about the 47-story tower allowed me to take a step back and slowly piece together the rest of the day's events.

The much-respected BBC newscast out of London, England, was conducting a report with *live* footage of Manhattan on a massive screen in the background. The ash cloud from the recently collapsed twin towers wasn't able to hide the image of building 7, still standing in the background. The problem? The BBC journalist reported that the building had already collapsed, and clearly, it hadn't yet. In London, the BBC network was provided with intelligence too early, which stood out like a sore thumb. It was sheer horror, unfolding in front of the eyes of the world. It was confusing, begging for clarity and resolution. The fact that holes exist proves inconsistency.

The Pentagon

After the initial shock from the news of another 'plane' slamming into the Pentagon, it was terrifying. As the events unfolded, I was already a bit suspicious, but when the video of the Pentagon damage started pouring in, once again, it just didn't make sense or add up to me.

American Airlines, Flight 77, the alleged aircraft to strike the Pentagon, uncovered the biggest magic illusion

A Cognitive Project

ever. After miraculously following a near impossible flight path, the Boeing 757 not only created a hole too small even to fit a commercial airliner of that size but somehow, none of the plane could be seen after impact. Airliners don't just disappear. Most air crashes will show signs of the massive engines, tail section, and fuselage in the debris field. They told us the plane 'vanished into the building. *Did they mean like a magic illusion or...?*

I have a problem with this part of the story because the Pentagon is the most secure and monitored building on the planet. It contains hundreds of CCTV surveillance cameras, yet the only footage they could show of the 'plane' making impact was blurry and from a distance. It doesn't look like a commercial airplane to me. It seems more like a missile, and the fact that other digital proof wasn't released to the general public, only strengthens the claims of a strategic and deliberate attack within.

Luckily, the Pentagon's west side in Arlington was conveniently undergoing renovations, and fatalities were limited, but the incident still claimed 125 men and women. Hard-working, innocent people with families, hopes and dreams. Again, it seemed as if science was going to debunk the official report, and the claims of truthers were making more sense than what they told us. It was becoming clear that we were all being lied to, and it wasn't over. The world was hooked into a soap opera.

The fact that experienced pilots with thousands of hours of flight experience testified that the maneuver needed by a commercial aircraft at those speeds and low altitudes just couldn't be done the way they reported it. Even the flight path failed to take down a feeble power pole before impact. Big plans are bound to have errors.

Small aircraft parts were littering the Pentagon's huge lawn, but the pieces, including a portion of landing gear, didn't seem to match that of a 757-passenger jet. Some were quick to point this out, along with the lack of digital proof, that based on the hole's sheer size, it wasn't very plausible that a third plane struck the Pentagon. Many agreed that the aircraft pieces were planted on the lawn to trick the general public and solidify their needs to support a quick and effective military strike on the enemy. Patriotism had finally been achieved, it seemed.

Flight 93 / Shanksville, Pennsylvania

As I mentioned earlier, when I saw the video of the 'plane' crash near Shanksville, I was convinced we were being lied to by someone. This one's tricky because the evidence of a crash is not present, but this was the most revered flight on this particular day. This was the flight that was supposedly heading toward the White House. The fourth hijacked fight in which the passengers stood together and rushed the cockpit, causing the jet to smash into the ground at supersonic speeds. Airplane disasters have ended like this in the past, and there is always evidence of significant aircraft debris. Even flights that crash into the sea reveal floating objects over time.

But we were told that the 'plane' hit the ground with such force that it disappeared below the soft earth. Most people nodded their heads and thought to themselves. *If that's what they told us, that must be what happened.* Even the Value Jet crash in 1996, which crashed in the Florida Everglades, offered a plethora of evidence after the accident. Aircraft just don't disintegrate into the mud.

They've even made a movie about Flight 93, and some have testified that they received cellular phone calls from the plane before its fatal descent. Remember, this was in 2001. Even today, it is next to impossible to connect a phone call from a jet at cruising altitude. But then I have to look at the personal accounts a bit closer. Flight 93, just like Flight 77 were registered and serving aircraft with real manifested passengers. If what I'm proposing is closer to the truth, what happened to the passengers? After a few more strange coincidences from that day, I'll give my opinion on the entire timeline, as grim as it may be. The sad part is that these events, although heavily reported on, lacked follow-up and arbitration. Conclusions were made and put down on paper before anyone was able to dispute the alleged facts officially. And now, these alleged facts will appear in children's textbooks, fooling our future generations.

Coincidences from that historical day

Few people know the strange coincidences that took place on September 11th, 2001. When these facts are thrown into the mix, you may be able to see how this day in history can be conceived in a whole different way.

- The US Airforce was very busy. They were training hard to ensure their free country was secure within. Consequently, they were training on hijacked aircraft and how to handle the situation. When the 'planes' were hijacked, air traffic control was confused, distinguishing the real hijacked airplanes and the ones being used for testing. NORAD was told to *stand down*, and no military jets were ever scrambled in the most sheltered country on the planet during a principal crisis in their history.

- Some of the nineteen hijackers took flying lessons right in the U.S.A. before the attacks. They would have had limited experience, and flying a jumbo jet is much different than a twin-engine airplane. The maneuvers need to hit the Pentagon were next to impossible, and it makes us question the validity of the claims as they were reported to us by the media. Even the low altitude, high-speed maneuver into the towers would need to be questioned as unachievable and completely untruthful.

- It was alleged that one of the hijacker's passports was discovered at ground zero. Please think about this for a minute. Even the steel melted from the fires. This seems to have been planted evidence, but I may be wrong. All of that fire and destruction should equal no passport.

- There were reports and photos distributed claiming that a piece of an engine from one of the 'planes' that struck the towers was found 'wedged' between two buildings below. The photo is quite fascinating. The engine piece doesn't resemble that of a large commercial jet, and at second glance, it's pretty simple to see a rope tied around the middle of it. This is only strange until you accept that the evidence was lowered with the rope and left for someone to discover. It appears to be some weak planted evidence, but they didn't think the idea through well.

- It became common knowledge that the senior Bin Laden family didn't like Osama too much. There are documented meetings, between George Bush and the Bin Laden family, before 9-11. In fact, after all airspace in North America had shut down that day, there is radar evidence of someone from the large Bin Laden family leaving American airspace and returning home to the Middle East. Osama may have been used as a martyr, and the family may have been paid millions of dollars for intelligence on oil sources deep in the Middle East. Records show many meetings leading up to that day.

- There are claims that many of the nineteen hijackers were discovered alive and living comfortably in their homes back in the east. That would make sense to me, as a complex operation like this would benefit highly by having a common enemy to strike back with retaliation.

Here's what I think happened on 9-11

If you haven't guessed by now, I believe that 9-11 was entirely an inside job. If you look back at American political history, this isn't a far stretch by any means. It took years to orchestrate this kind of a plan, and it all started years before, in 1990, when Iraq invaded Kuwait. The rest of the story follows a precise and forthright timeline that should show proof of their motivation.

Muslim extremists were a clear focal point for the former President, George H.W. Bush. (Senior) We can all remember his retaliation onto the streets of Bagdad in 1990/1991, during the brutal Gulf War, demonstrating America's aggressive military capabilities in response to Iraq's attack on oil-rich Kuwait. The footage on TV was quite alarming, showing real-time obliteration of Iraq.

When George W. Bush took power, his father had some unfinished business he wished his son to complete. It was a huge opportunity to take a stranglehold on the world's oil industry and claim a stronger dominance on the faltering American economy. But Bush Jr. needed a reason to go back to the Middle East. He couldn't send troops over in force, as his people would rebel and argue the lack of diplomacy. I believe this was when the ball started rolling on 9-11. *Create a common enemy, and it would be like taking candy from a baby*, they thought. They would simply include a foreign power to support their cause. The master plan was conceived without considering all of the complex consequences and the scientific variances. No one would ever know.

Fast-forward to that fateful day, and I will admit that I do believe some sort of 'aircraft' did hit the towers. As I had mentioned, I was skeptical at first, but if it weren't an internal blast like many had claimed, the following would make sense of what actually caused the damage.

The American military has always been a world leader in weaponry. They are continually preparing some state-of-the-art technologies with the deadliest, pinpoint accuracy within their arsenal. The problem was that the United States hadn't been in an armed conflict in a while, and contrary to popular belief, war is good for the economy, creating thousands of jobs for the redundant.

I think it's possible that the government manipulated two commissioned airline jets and fixed them with a potential experimental weapon within the nose cones. A type of compacted missile, if you will. If this was the case, it could explain how the 'plane' was able to pass through the steel beams and even explode out the other side of the structure, as the video shows quite clearly. The passengers wouldn't have seen it coming, but it seems unlikely that the pilots were held at bay in the cockpit by men holding box cutters to their throats.

The explosions would have ripped through, deep into the structure's floors (ceilings and walls), and there was more than enough fuel to keep the fires raging, but those buildings should not have collapsed the way they did. Lives would have been lost either way, but that was silly.

I believe the weeks leading up to September eleventh allowed contractors to wire the building, floor by floor and cut central support beams to weaken them. Even a controlled demolition has many precise processes.

When the time was right, I believe the detonation brought both towers down, causing the most dramatic scenes of death and desperation. Thermite explosives were used, and this is the only thing that can explain the 'molten metal' running down the severed columns at ground zero. That was the number one ingredient used.

Even the evil conductors of this vile and selfish plan couldn't have imagined what would happen after that. The countless fires that started and the suffocating ash from the concrete, and other smashed substrates, caused noxious respiratory issues that still plague some of those that were affected today. The recovery and the cleanup were completed as fast as possible but not fast enough to hide some telltale signs of corruption. This would unite the States in a way they hadn't felt in decades, if not longer. Destroy the enemy, and create a relatable bond.

While this was happening in New York, I believe that another experimental weapon hit the Pentagon as part of the elaborate plan. The world was already convinced that aircraft had struck the twin towers, so announcing that another flight had struck the Pentagon was very easy to believe and only strengthened terrorism arguments.

The sad fact that the American government couldn't offer sufficient proof that an airplane hit the building was the smoking gun here. The hole wasn't big enough, and the flight path was impossible to negotiate by an amateur and professional pilot alike. If nothing else, take the Pentagon incident as a clue to how they lied to us. Most of the events on that day were misreported. I believe they made a massive error with the 'crash' in Pennsylvania.

From the cell phone discrepancies to the passengers' heroic story fighting back, there is something that just can't be denied. Both scientifically and logically, we can't believe a commercial passenger aircraft crashed there. Like the buildings in New York collapsing, air disasters have never looked like that before, and we have to believe that if something *hasn't* happened before, or since, it's improbable to have occurred on that day.

It looks like another missile or experimental weapon was fired into the ground and precisely targeted. The land's topography around the impact zone was similar to an airplane's shape on its belly with its wings exposed to the sides. You can go to Google Earth and see the same pareidolia case in the field, even today.

If this wasn't enough, they detonated Building 7, back in New York, to destroy any evidence compiled for their plan, as well as the many lies and secrets from history.

The 9-11 Commission assembled a report, and very little on the civil trials were ever released to the general public. A court ruling accepted the vague testimony and the 9-11 Commission's report became the 'gospel' that we all accepted worldwide. Truth be known, 9-11 became the biggest scam ever conceived. The United States people accepted a 'War on Terrorism' and lobbied the military to take action overseas. Their motivation and overwhelming influence caused a crushing death toll, including many peace-loving civilians in the Middle East. This toll included women and even young children.

In all, 9-11 cost an initial total of 2,996 deaths. There were many more deaths, after the fact, from respiratory illness and mental instability could be expected for life. Make no mistake, this was an act of terrorism, and it was a deliberate and well-executed plot, but it backfired.

The wars in Iraq and Afghanistan killed another 10,000 plus American's, and these numbers continue to rise today. In all, more than 800,000 people have been killed and 37 million people displaced. You can do the math and see who won, but what victory was achieved?

I may be way out to lunch on this opinion, and I'm not saying I'm correct, but by considering everything, it can become a memory that has some closure. Closure, which I hope has been obtained by the victims' families from September eleventh, 2001. A sad day for humanity.

Pentagon Disclaimer

The television program *Mayday* reconstructs air crashes, and the NTSB makes recommendations so they will never happen again. In the Pentagon episode, they explain the story precisely as it was reported. What caught my ear during that episode was when an aviation analyst was interviewed and says, in response to why little of the aircraft could be found at the scene. *"When you have an airplane hitting pretty much solid brick, it just vaporizes; there's not a lot left."* That's something to keep in mind when we ponder the story of the same kind of jet passing through two *steel* buildings earlier that day.

"He could tell by the way animals walked that they were keeping time to some kind of music. Maybe it was the song in their own hearts that they walked to."

— Laura Adams Armer

A Cognitive Project

Amazing Animal Encounters

Okay, it's time to take a couple of steps back from the controversial and all of the conspiracy theories. Here's an opportunity for some fun and a chance for you to play a simple game with me during this chapter. Not everything you've been told by news sources and social media is true. We know this, but sometimes we decide that the story we're told will be accepted because the truth may be too tricky to decipher. We make a choice, and we may be passing our false information to others.

This chapter is a way to prove how easy it is to fool you and cause you to believe something that isn't necessarily the truth. I'll share ten short stories during this section. Each will be three to five pages long. Eight of the ten stories will be actual encounters that I've had with the animal kingdom in my life. Two of the stories will be fictional accounts from my imagination and told similarly. You can choose what to believe and what not.

Your job is to see if you can distinguish factual stories from fictional tales. In this case, you have the advantage of knowing that I will be honest with you. I have altered the names in the reports so you don't gain an advantage but be assured, eight of the following were unique experiences for me. Good luck, and let the game begin.

I

Wicca and the Waxwings

It was an early, cold February afternoon. The landscape outside was blinding to the eye from the recent snowfall, blanketing the lawn, trees and bushes around Stan's property. Each flake reflected the radiant sun, sending light in all directions. But at least it wasn't too chilly outside. That in itself was a blessing for the time of year.

Stan opened his sliding glass door from his master bedroom. He sipped a cup of coffee and felt the chill in the air while glaring at his shabby, rust-coloured deck. Maybe he would completely rebuild it and get rid of the solid wall running along the front. It was four feet high and an absolute waste of possibilities. Maybe he could add some stairs. As he thought of his needs to repair the eyesore, something much more prolific commanded his attention. It was an audible noise, and Stan couldn't remember ever hearing such a fantastic racket in his life.

It was the sound of birds. But not just a few birds. It was the sound of hundreds of birds, and as Stan lifted his head, he could see them all swarming the large Dogwood tree fixed in the corner of the back yard. They screamed, and their chirps came in an overlapping procession.

They weren't the common Sparrows that inhabited the trees around the yard year-round. They were larger birds, and Stan recognized them from their distinct markings. The Waxwings had arrived at a strange time of year, and they were frantic. The gigantic branches had saved some spoiled berry bunches that hung throughout the tree and hadn't fallen to the ground yet. That was what the birds searched for themselves. They had arrived with a vengeance to have a feast before moving on.

The sound from the many birds was powerful, and one couldn't help but pay attention to the magical display. Each unique bird had two trademark patterns with yellow tail feathers and Cardinal-shaped heads. As Stan took a step out into the snow build-up on the deck, he looked to his right and caught something out of his peripheral vision, approaching from behind him. He turned his head to see his old companion, Wicca, who was alert to the familiar sounds coming from the trees.

Wicca was their adored family pet. A domesticated, short-haired, pure black cat, Wicca was in the twilight of her life, having just turned eighteen years old in October. She was in good health still, but Stan and his family knew that the time she had left was short. She had always been the Queen of the locality and defended her territory like a vicious lioness, gaining her a daunting reputation. She had shuffled her way to the back exit and peered out.

Stan just watched as Wicca made her way to the solid front wall on the deck, shielding her from the tree above in the backyard's distance. She listened intently as the birds kept arriving, and each played their song. It was an announcement of a splendid murder if you asked Stan.

The waxwings were clearing the berries and ensuring to clean up any that had fallen too. As they shrieked loudly, more would arrive, and it wouldn't take long for them to move on. Wicca raised her tired eyes and started her way to the end of the deck, where a small set of stairs allowed access to the back lawn. Stan just watched and connected with the fact that Wicca had now shown her predatory traits, looking at a meal for herself.

The commotion continued, and as Wicca turned her head around the wall, the most amazing thing happened. The birds became immediately silent. Each one of them stopped chirping at precisely the same time. The ones in flight landed and stood like statues, and the one's on the ground froze and stared at the cat's form. Wicca didn't advance. She stopped when the birds did and glared at the tree, craving for more motion and sound. But the birds were highly gifted, and they had instinctually prepared for moments like this. They continued to stay quiet, and none of them flew away. Stan watched in disbelief, shifting his head from the tree to the cat and back again. It would remind him of an authentic Mexican

Standoff, and somehow, it now had appeared as if the attractive birds were going to triumph over the cat.

Sure enough, after three or four moments, Wicca had lost interest and was quite inconvenienced by the cold snow on her feet, so she turned and made her way back into the house. Stan then watched as the birds all bailed from the tree and headed east and away from his sight. They didn't make another sound, and at once, they were gone. Their bizarre interaction would never occur again.

Stan realized at that moment that the animal kingdom hid many secrets. As soon as the birds saw the cat, they could silence themselves within a precise second. The mystery behind their motivation would remain intact, much longer than Wicca herself, who would cross the rainbow bridge in the summer of the following year. But the humble house cat was able to teach a valuable lesson.

Every animal on our planet wants to live, and most will do anything to continue their survival. There will always be predators, and there will always be prey. But if nature has taught us anything, it's that a species' lifespan is just as much dependent on the animal's intelligence as the fortitude of the assembly surrounding it. Strength in numbers has the same equivalent value, no matter what species evolve and roam our regal planet. They all have just as much right to be here as we do.

II

Black Bear on the Camp Path

The vast wilderness in Northern British Columbia was absolutely astounding. For Sheldon, a first-year tree planter, it was an adventure that few would be able to experience. The smells and the sights brought him some freedom and allowed him to open his mind. Tall pines and plenty of foliage would invite many different insects and small rodents to show up in abundance. But some dangerous animals also called this area their home, and Sheldon was well aware of their presence on the range. After all, this was their habitat, and Sheldon was a guest.

Sheldon was making his way back to his temporary camp, down the path of the western cutline. He was alone, and this was something that was shunned upon by the supervisors. Foremen suggested that planters always worked in pairs. But this was the end of the day, and Sheldon's partner had been feeling sick from drinking the muddy water from a weeded slew days earlier. After lunch, he had headed back to camp, but Sheldon wasn't about to waive his payment for the day by not working. He, too, had drunk some of the dirty water, as it was all they had. His stomach rolled a bit, but he was exhausted, and he wanted to rest. He shuffled his feet in the dirt and lowered his head to look at the ground. *Just ten more minutes*, he thought. Then he could fill his angry belly.

The weather was calm, and there was a slight breeze rolling over the hilltops, creating a gentle hum. Sheldon carried his sharp planting spade and a triple-pocketed planting bag around his waist and over his shoulders. Thankfully, they were finally empty, for when they were full, they carried more than five hundred saplings and weighed upwards of forty-five pounds. The immense pressure around his neck stretches his tendons, but he pushed through it every day. Failure wasn't an option.

Appreciating the walk and taking in the aromas of the wildflowers and pines, Sheldon walked over a small hill on the path, and he felt the air around him change. He slowly lifted his head, snapping it to the left, where he would come, face to face, with a large, wild black bear.

Sheldon loved the bear as an animal. He had studied them and knew all of their species and habitats. The young man hoped to see one during his stay at this particular camp but couldn't have imagined such a surprise encounter. He stood, with his mouth wide open, and the bear glared back, no more than four feet away.

It was then that Sheldon realized he needed to pee. The urge had become more assertive when he saw the beast in front of him. His mind raced, and a mere twenty-second adventure would last for hours in his head. His lip quivered, and the bear wasn't happy that Sheldon had arrived on the scene. It made some low grunting noises.

The majestic creature wouldn't move, but Sheldon hoped it was just as scared of him as he was of it. The frightened first-year planter took a few steps back and contemplated his options. He knew, from his research, that he shouldn't run, as it could trigger the bear to attack. Sheldon was well aware that all of the 'bad' bears from the National parks were moved up north. These would be the bears that had unsafe human contact in the past.

Sheldon turned his head, keeping his eyes on the bear. He looked around for a tree to climb, but the area had been clear-cut and only offered weak and gangly options. As his urge to urinate grew stronger, Sheldon became feeble in the knees. He then realized his mortality.

After a couple more steps away, his hand became numb, and he dropped his shovel, making the bear bow to the sudden noise. Sheldon had dropped his only weapon, should the bear decide to advance, and now his options were limited. He thought of playing dead, but the three-year-old female black bear had a different idea.

The bear kept its eyes connected with Sheldon and reared up to show its dominance. But before Sheldon could react, the animal bolted to the right, running at full speed away from the scene. It galloped over a large hill and into the cut-line to the east. Sheldon was breathing quickly. He waited for thirty seconds and picked up his shovel again. *I could be dead,* he thought to himself.

Slowly, Sheldon's curiosity had gotten the best of him. He tempted his fate and advanced on the hill to see where the bear had ended up. It may have been waiting for him, but he remained intrigued and made it to the crest of the hill. He couldn't see the bear at first glance, which brought anxiety back, but then he spotted it.

The giant bear had made it across the cut-line and into the eastern trees in less than thirty seconds. Sheldon could see it slowly crashing through the bush, and he was able to breathe correctly again. He was all alone and finally relieved himself on the parched, crusted dirt.

Sheldon continued down the path, and a smile crossed his lips. He was still so tired, but now his adrenaline ruled, and he ensured to turn and look down the trail many times for the rest of the walk. He couldn't wait to get back and tell his co-workers about his experience, but he hoped the hungry bear wasn't following him home.

Once he was safe, Sheldon finally stopped shaking. He had experienced something that few do in the wild, and he knew that it could have turned out completely different. Perhaps the story would have never been told.

III

The Invisible Prey

It was only four days until Christmas. A crisp but clear Saturday morning had invited a group of teenaged boys to get together and explore the frozen landscape. Seth led the group. He was a bossy, fourteen-year-old who looked at bullying as a privilege and practiced it often. The others were Seth's younger brother, Dan, and a couple of loyal followers named Bradley and Ronny.

The boys had made their way to the outskirts of town, trudging through the deep snow and playing childish games along their journey. Their amusement was easily achieved, and as long as everyone followed Seth's lead, there would never be significant issues within the group.

They approached a tall, chain-linked fence with thick barbed wire adorning the top of it, and it ran for miles separating the Northside of town from the farmlands and fields. For some reason, Seth was interested in the fence and challenged the others to climb over to the other side's private property. Dan was against it right away, but Ronny said he would do it, even with the barbed wire threat in the way. Bradley wasn't too interested and was a law-abiding young man. But he knew that if he wanted to be part of their 'cool' group, he needed to show some interest, so he did. Seth gave Ronny a nudge toward the fence, and the rest of the boys cheered him on.

Dan tried to talk Seth out of it, but it appeared too late, as Ronny had gripped the fence and made a few false steps with his feet. The boys became silent and watched as their friend started to climb, and to Bradley, it seemed that every adventure had a hint of danger attached to it. Ronny only made it about halfway up before losing his grip, and he came falling back into a deep snowbank.

After the laughter had subsided, it was Bradley who looked up to the horizon and commanded everyone's attention, pointing into the distance at something in the clear, vast sky. Everyone stopped what they were doing and followed his stare, questioning the distraction.

It was hard to make out at first, but it flew with an imposing presence, and as it got closer to them, it had become apparent. It was a massive Snowy Owl, and it was flying toward them, getting more prominent in the sky with each flap of its wings. Seth had turned away. It wasn't captivating to him, but the others riveted their attention to the enormous bird in the sky. They had never seen such a fantastic sight in the wild. Snowy owls just weren't commonly seen, especially this close to the town limits. It had a purpose, and Bradley was in awe.

The boys scouted the fields below, as it appeared the owl was preparing to land in the snow-covered grounds, piercing its wings back and extending its enormous talons. Maybe it had spotted a mouse or an injured, smaller bird. As it got closer, the boys could see the sheer size of the owl, and it was making its grand entrance only thirty feet away. Dan yelled, "Shit, it's coming for us."

The boys fixated on the descent but weren't prepared for what they were about to witness. The grand owl, white as the glistening snow, smashed into the snow-covered ground with a tremendous but controlled force. Almost as soon as it landed, it had propelled itself back into the sky with a few swipes of its wings, measuring a good five feet across. In its mighty talons hung a giant jack-rabbit. The enormous hare was just as white as the owl and measured a solid three feet from the tips of its ears to its dangling hind feet. It wasn't going to escape.

The rabbit had accepted its fate as the owl flew away toward the Earth's curvature and was never seen again by the boys. Seth was preoccupied with finding their next adventure, but the others truly felt they had witnessed something extraordinary. They couldn't see the hefty rabbit, but the owl could, and it would waste no time feeding its instincts in the wild. Nature displayed the circle of life to them at a young age, and they would learn from their experiences, just as the owl and the rabbit did.

IV

The Centennial Horror

Every summer, for five years straight, the boys and girls in the neighbourhood would all meet in the Centennial field for a friendly game of flag football. Usually, the same bunch would come out and play, but the group welcomed newcomers every once in a while. More people would make the game competitive.

The Centennial grounds were huge and offered ample space for the children to find adventure. There was an Elementary school, a playground with many amenities, like two ball diamonds, and a full-sized football field running down the center. The kids would never miss an opportunity to get together while the weather was mild.

One of the participants, Blaine, lived only a couple of blocks away from the field. He knew the area well, and the surrounding properties housed some friends to Blaine. They had all lived in the neighbourhood for some time now. Living behind the north baseball diamond was an older couple who owned a sweet little dog. Its name was Benji, and they would often let the tiny Shih-Tzu out of the back gate to frolic and beg for attention from the boys and girls while they played. But the house behind the south diamond was mysterious. They seldom saw the owners, and their back entrance was adorned with a seven-foot wooden fence and an oval swinging gate. It was there for a reason as they, too, owned a dog. This canine, however, was dangerous and rarely seen. Its name was Sarge, a full-grown, black Doberman Pincher. Most children would choose to play ball on the north diamond, as the south one had an uncomfortable feel to it and wasn't preferred if they had a choice to make.

Blaine had joined the others at mid-field, and they picked teams, as per usual. Once they had chosen their assignments and strapped on their coloured flags to their waists, the game was underway. The children would run and pass the football, advancing down the field and back again until they needed to rest. As they huddled and drank their water, the gate behind the north baseball diamond opened, and the sweet lady who resided there waved as Benji came running to join in the jubilation.

The children went back to their game and welcomed Benji as another player. The small dog would bolt, back and forth, up and down the field, and the boys and girls had to be careful not to trip over her. She stayed out with them for nearly an hour, and the children were taking another break before finishing up the game for the day. They drank their water and laughed at Benji, who was hopping around and begging for attention from the kids.

This time they sat in a circle, and Benji bounded back and forth between them. She was such a lovable dog and allowed the children who didn't have a pet to rejoice. As the break ended and Blaine got to his feet, he caught something out of the corner of his eye. It was the back gate behind the south diamond, and sure enough, Sarge had strutted through, waving his nose in the air. The gate slowly closed behind him, and the owners never showed their faces. Sarge started to gradually make his way to the location of the football field, and everyone noticed.

They decided to ignore the big dog and proceed with the fourth quarter of their contest, but it was then that all hell broke loose. A small field rabbit had made its way onto the pitch, and it was a young girl who first pointed it out. It had wanted to join the game as well but little did the little rabbit know; it had stumbled upon perilous land.

Benji noticed the bunny, and then the chase was on. The rabbit zig-zagged around the field with Benji in hot pursuit. The little dog was fast, but the rabbit was agile, bobbing left and right, toying with the old pup.

On his way over, Sarge also noticed and stood tall with his ears pointed to the sky. The stubby-tailed canine bolted forward, seeing the rabbit himself, and looked like a Greyhound in posture while it ran. Now there were two hounds in pursuit, and the rabbit was outnumbered.

The children were astonished as they watched from their circle. No one was even willing to get involved, and nature seemed to be stemming its course once again.

Now Sarge had caught up, and he too made sharp turns in the target of the tiny rabbit, but Benji was starting to lose ground. She was falling behind as the rabbit made a sharp 180-degree turn and bolted back toward the kids. It was able to avoid Sarge's first strike.

Benji had tried to follow and seemed to have gained a second wind. The rabbit, too, was exhausted and was losing a step on the two pursuing dogs. After one more turn, Benji was only a couple of feet away from her first catch, but before she could claim victory, it was over.

It ended quickly, and as the rabbit bounced away, the children began to shake and were speechless. Sarge looked down at his fresh kill. He had snapped the gentle dog's neck, and there was no blood. Blaine made his way to the small dog's corpse as soon as Sarge had walked away and back to his house behind the south diamond.

Some of the children cried. As the others surrounded the lifeless white dog, Blaine looked up to see where Sarge had gone. The tall wooden gate was open, just a crack, and the Doberman walked through and out of sight. The gate closed with the distinctive click of the latch, and they would never forget the horror at the park.

V

Elk on the Highway

Kirk and Marko were painting a house on the outskirts of town. The owner had promised a tidy sum for a completed job, and two friends knew it would be easy money. They would have it done in one day and enjoy some beers that evening, back in the comfort of home.

They were blessed to live in one of the most beautiful places in the world. Northern Vancouver Island was often taken for granted by the many friendly residents, but to visit, you would proclaim it to be '*God's country.*' With the mighty Pacific Ocean on its doorstep, the Island would harbour all sorts of marine life, from Orcas to Seals, and the best salmon fishing in the entire world.

The two men took Kirk's little Mazda 232 to the site, and they had prepped their supplies the night before. It was hot outside, and the guys would have to sweat the day out with a temperature of thirty-two degrees Celsius. They got started and stayed at it for six hours straight. The house overlooked the sea and was now a new shade of green. Marko congratulated Kirk on a job well done. Now they could pack up and drive over to the cold beer store before heading back to Kirk's house for a steak.

Happy with their successful duties done, the two men sped back on the inland island highway. Kirk drove his compact car, as the ocean presented itself to his left, and a crowning tower of Spruce trees to his right. Kirk was heeding the speed limit, which was posted at ninety km. Both were wearing their sturdy shoulder seatbelts.

Kirk then noticed something moving on the road's shoulder to his right and well ahead about halfway back home. He hovered over his brake and eventually had to apply some brake pressure, as he now saw his obstacle.

It was a full-grown female Elk, and Kirk, for one had never seen something so astonishing before, live and right in front of him. He watched, along with Marko, and Kirk had slowed enough to allow the huge deer to cross safely. But a fair distance away, the danger became real.

Kirk was enthralled with the elk, which was easily the size of a horse. He still hovered over the break and slowed the little Mazda to thirty-five kilometres an hour. But as Kirk watched the elk cross into the left trees, Marko still watched the road, and he had a dire warning.

"KIRK, THERE'S ANOTHER ONE!" He screamed the statement at the top of his lungs and commanded his friend's attention. Kirk instinctively turned his head as he slammed down on his brakes. There, following its mother, was her calf, and it was the size of a sturdy pony.

The small car reared forward, and all of the weight shifted to the dash. It felt like the car went up on its front wheels, but now within twenty feet of the baby, the breaks weren't going to stop them in time. Marko's life flashed in front of his eyes, and the young elk stopped in the middle of the lane, staring blankly at the vehicle.

It had happened so fast, but as the Mazda finally slowed to around eight kilometres an hour, it made an impact with the elk, taking out its long legs and causing it to collapse on the hood of the car, as it finally stopped.

The young elk bounced off the front of the car, and the hood popped, along with the entire frame of the vehicle. It ran off to meet its mother again, waiting on the other side, and Kirk shook, flicking on his hazard lights and pulling his car off to the side of the road. He wasn't even able to drive anymore without gaining his bearings, but the experience was authentic, and only seconds would have stopped the elk from going through the windshield of the compact car. Luck was definitely on their sides, and they would be given another chance.

If it weren't for Marko's brash warning, Kirk would have slammed into the elk at more than sixty kilometres an hour. Both men would have likely been killed, but it wasn't their time, and the regal elk could continue living in paradise. The animals had taught yet another lesson.

VI

Murderous Monkeys

Travelling to Europe was a special treat for Leigh. For the first time, he had voyaged overseas and had two months to travel through the many small countries and visit relatives located in the United Kingdom. One of Leigh's many hopes was to visit the famous London Zoo.

The weekend would allow Leigh to collect many special memories of the historic London area, and in the afternoon, they would make their way to the famed zoo. Leigh would look forward to seeing the bears, tigers, and monkeys, in particular. The monkeys were so amusing.

After visiting many of the exhibits and eating a copious amount of junk food, Leigh made his way to the massive spider monkey cage. He was fortunate to stand as close to the cage as possible. He had the perfect view of the funny little mammals but was surprised that such a large area only housed two of the humorous creatures.

The cage was full of exotic, natural plants and bushes. There were rocks and artificial watering holes, but the pen itself stood as a pinnacle of security. The holes were reasonably small, and there was reinforced steel on all of the openings. Leigh was mindful that monkeys could be dangerous, but the zoo's staff were chiefly and rightfully concerned for their guest's safety and enjoyment.

Leigh watched the two monkeys swinging from their natural branches, screaming with a deafening shriek at times, and igniting the crowd with laughter. Then, something had caught Leigh's eye in the cage's corner.

It was a bird, and it was a fair size. Leigh wasn't sure what sort of bird it was, but it had made its way into the cage somehow and flapped its wings, gaining attention. And then there were two. Two birds of the same species flew from the corner of the coop and circled the enclosure in a holding pattern. By now, the two spider monkeys had noticed, and their curiosity wasn't good news for the birds. The crowds were cheering as the monkeys jumped and swung, chasing the birds around their cage, but their cheers would soon change to moans.

It was apparent that the monkeys weren't there to play with the birds. They were now the predators, and the watching tourists were about to see a scary 'circle of life' moment. The birds were starting to tire out, and Leigh scanned the cage for the hole they must have entered through. *Why weren't they just going back to that hole?*

But Leigh didn't understand that the birds weren't able to figure it out. They just flew in circles trying to flee the deadly monkeys, and they had no options.

Leigh watched in shock now as the helpless birds had all but given up. They just didn't have the strength to flee anymore. Sadness would soon overcome Leigh, and he scanned the area for a zookeeper to intervene and release the birds from the cage. But it was too late. The monkeys hadn't slowed down, and they were able to navigate with great precision. The crowd braced for vicious carnage.

Sure enough, the smaller female monkey trapped one of the birds in the far corner of the cage. The bird had surrendered, and the monkey's instincts had kicked in. Its long arms reached out and grabbed the helpless bird before ripping its head away from its body in one horrendous motion causing the crowd to shriek in horror.

The monkeys themselves became more boisterous and summoned more visitors to the cage. They were just in time to see the second destitute bird get captured by the larger male. The bird cried mercy as the monkey held it tight, but it didn't seem to want to harm the bird.

The female, noticing her mate's catch, dropped her feathered corpse and hustled over to him. The female was ferocious, and as Leigh and the others watched in disgust, she grabbed one of the poor birds' longs wings. The male held tight to the other wing, and like a turkey's wishbone, the unfortunate bird was ripped in half. Leigh would remember this chilling moment for eternity.

VII

The Cookshack Shooting

Summer camp was specifically important this year. The children were all heading into the Rocky Mountains this trip, and for most, it was their first time in the wilderness. They would set up some temporary living quarters and a massive cookshack where the kids would enjoy their meals from a camp cook, ready to provide breakfast, lunch and supper with a variety of healthy meal choices for all. They certainly spared no expense.

This year, there were twenty-six children enrolled in the week-long educational experience. They would learn basic survival techniques and absorb how to live off the land if need be. All participants would have to sign a waiver, as the Jasper National Park was a hotbed for wild animals. From Wolves to Cougars, and Grizzley Bears.

The boys and girls had only been camping for two days and had already encountered some sheep and many wildflowers distinguishing the majestic scenery. They lined up to enter the meal tent only an hour before their nightly campfire to partake in a feast of Lasagna, Garlic Toast and Caesar Salad. By the time they finished eating, twilight would approach, and the fire would soon begin.

Two men and two women counselled the activities and were all experienced educators, having loads of knowledge in the vast wilderness. The head counsellor's name was Larry. He was a kind, gentle man who had compassion and patience with the children. Everyone could tell that he took his job seriously and made the children's safety his top priority. Larry was a tall and skilled man in his early forties who counselled part-time.

Once everyone had made it through the meal line, one of the children, Glen was wincing, as he was bitten by a large horsefly while waiting for his lasagna. He sat with his friends at the back of the tent and showed off his wound while holding back tears from the painful bite.

As time healed, Glen could cope with his discomfort and swallowed back the delicious pasta, along with his campmates. Once everyone had finished, they would help cleaning up their area before heading to the fire.

It was then that some of the children, including Glen, would be scarred for life with an etched memory. As the conversation mellowed, an uninvited guest showed up at the entrance flaps of the cook tent. It was a large black bear, and it had simply been walking through its territory when it smelled the aromas of the meat and cheese. This bear wasn't afraid, and that posed an immediate danger. Everyone reacted with shock and held their breath.

The large male black bear swayed its head back and forth, lifting its bulky nose high in the air to confirm its suspicions. It was a tense situation that lasted for only a couple of minutes, but some kids were now crying and afraid for their lives. Many had never seen a wild animal of that size, so close, including young Glen.

After one more glance at the camp's cook, the bear backed away and walked the perimeter of the tent, sniffing the fabric for a safer place to enter. Ordinarily, the bear should have been frightened away by the sheer number of intruders, but this bear was hungry, and nothing was going to drive it to another location. Larry took the opportunity to flee from the cookshack, and he bolted off to his living quarters, leaving the children and the other counsellors to fend for themselves.

The bear had completed one round of the cook tent, wallowing by the entrance again without re-entering, but the children could still see the beast. Even with their screams and dire warnings, the children wouldn't deter the animal. It looked as if it would move on and strolled ten feet away, then stopped and turned its head back.

Larry had soon returned, brandishing a long rifle. He dipped into the tent and made the already panicked children cry out with a new fear. Many of them had never seen a firearm before. Larry loaded a shot into the cavity.

And then Glen had realized that it wasn't a rifle at all. And it wasn't a bullet he had loaded into the gun. It was a shell, and Larry was wielding a shotgun. Larry creeped out of the tent, and even though the other counsellors were adamant about the kids staying put, their curiosity was too intense, and they made their way to the flaps to follow the action and get another look at the bear.

Glen was the first in line, and as soon as he exited the tent, Larry had scoped his trophy and fired a blaring shot at the retreating bear. The children screamed in horror and pleaded for Larry to stop his assault, but he was too far gone. He pointed the weapon at the wounded bear, who took some of the pellets. After a second shot, the kind bear rolled as it tried to run away from the pain.

Larry reloaded and took a few steps forward, pointing the shotgun at the bear again. The children continued to implore for the attack to come to an end, but it only got worse. The third shot rang out, with everyone witness, and finally dropped the massive bear, succumbing to its many bloody wounds. But it hadn't died yet and lied in a pool of its body fluids. Larry approached the bear one last time and put the fourth shell into its head, thankfully killing it instantly. It happened so fast and was horrible.

Some of the children came closer, but others cowered by the cookshack and were seemingly traumatized. Glen was saddened. He knew that Larry probably had to do what he did, but the fact that it took four shots bothered him for some reason. *Was the pain inflicted on the bear necessary?* It was such a confusing time during an educational outing. This wasn't what they signed up for.

Later that evening, after things had calmed down, the group did end up sitting around their cozy campfire. Some of the kids had requested to go home, but this wouldn't be possible until daylight, so the counsellors tried to keep everyone calm and ensure their safety, even after the earlier events. They managed to carry on with a narrative that stayed positive through the night, but just as they were getting ready to retire for the evening, Larry decided to make a bold confession to the campmates.

Triumphantly, Larry spoke about his heroic kill. He was a bit embarrassed when describing his reloading skills. It would be the next piece of news that made Glen sick to his stomach, and he surely wasn't the only one. Larry casually mentioned that his shotgun was loaded with 'birdshot.' A round casing with many miniature bearings, specifically made to shoot birds out of the air. The bear had suffered greatly, and unfortunately, on this camping trip, the experience was nothing for Glen or his campmates to write home about. But the unforgettable sound of the deadly shots as they echoed would never leave their dented memories for as long as they lived.

VIII

Moose Suicide

Darnell and his family were travelling through the Rogers Pass in his father's 1972 brown Mercury. It was a beautiful day, as Darnell and his older sister, Emily was attentive to the possibility of seeing a wild animal while touring through the vast mountain ranges of Canada. Emily, though, was starting to doze off. She was up the earliest that morning and couldn't keep her eyes open.

There were many twists and turns throughout the route, and even a couple of dark tunnels, passing right through the mighty rock faces. Darnell glued his face into the window of the backseat. He would pass the time counting the cars and keeping track of the colours in his head to see the most popular. White always won, it seemed. *Why were there so many white cars?*

As Darnell's father rounded a corner amid the ranges, his mother screamed out to stop the car, as there seemed to be some sort of construction or accident ahead. Emily was suddenly wide awake again, asking her mother what the delay was. Stopping on the highway was a no, no, and they peered back at the growing line of traffic behind them. Everyone waited, and the line of cars didn't budge.

A Cognitive Project

Darnell lowered his window. (An act that had him scolded by his mother) and poked his head out to see down the road better. He saw some people outside of their cars, walking in different directions and paying close attention to something at the scene. It must be a car accident, as they suspected, but soon it would become abundantly clear what was happening at that moment.

The deep bend in the road rose above a massive cliff, full of tall Spruces and Pines. There was a sharp, metal guardrail bending around the outside of the highway. It was a safety precaution for the vehicles in case of a mishap. Now everyone had lowered their windows and could hear some voices in the commotion ahead. *Jesus*, Darnell's father thought, *someone's gone over the rail*.

More people, just in front of the families Mercury, were leaving their safe vehicles. There was something significant, happening and it provoked Darnell and his family to leave the security of their car as well. It was then that the situation became very real for all involved.

Walking on the side of the highway was an incredible sight. It was an adult Bull Moose, and it had a rack of horns on it that Darnell could have easily laid across comfortably. It was stressed, and people were baffled as to how it got to where it was. There were sheer cliffs to the right of the highway and the drop-off to the left.

Many took photographs, and some were even trying to feed the gentle giant. But the moose wanted no part of it. The large deer galloped down the side of the highway toward Darnell's car and then turned back again. It was shaking its terrific head as saliva flew from its snout.

The family stood close to their car again as the action took place within twenty-five feet of their location. The tourist became even more persistent, moving closer and closer to the moose to get the perfect photo. But Darnell could sense that something awful was going to happen. Even at fourteen years of age, his head told him that this situation wasn't going to end well for the kind animal.

He was correct as, with little warning at all, the moose slipped on the pavement, its hooves clacking down the road and hopped over the metal rail with little effort. He now stood, precariously, on the side of the cliff. But even this didn't deter some of the curious travellers. They continued their advance on the defenceless creature, and before everyone's eyes, it decided to leap from the cliff's edge, disappearing out of their sight altogether.

The crashes of the dense foliage below could be heard snapping violently, and it appeared the moose had taken its own life in the end. Darnell and his family were speechless, but they got back into the car and waited for the traffic to clear before proceeding down the highway.

IX

Shithead on the Farm

The Frederick Arm could be the most beautiful place on the planet, thought Jesper. The cozy inlet was set in the Pacific Ocean on the pristine British Columbia coast, just off Vancouver Island. Jesper was a lucky man, having secured a position with an affluent company in the aquaculture industry. He would spend six days in camp and six long days back at home. It was a pretty good work/home balance, and it paid the bills on time.

The salmon farms in British Columbia would face environmental scrutiny every single day that they were operating. Ignorant politicians weren't paying attention to science and making faulty assumptions that were not only negligent but un-educated and threatening to many who relied on the industry to feed their loving families.

Jesper was happy to work out in the fresh air. Yes, there were times that the winds would push you to the limits, and the rain would pound down, sideways at times. But when it was tranquil, there was nothing, anywhere like it. His many duties included conducting environmental testing, feeding the hordes of young salmon, accepting the feed deliveries, and cleanliness.

Jesper worked with three others during his shift, and the senior member's name was Yarley. Yarley was a grizzled veteran of Norwegian descent who had worked at the various farms in the region for more than twenty years. He was an expert in knots and made sure that all of the fish pens and predator nets were stitched proper and repaired frequently. Yarely was a mentor to Jesper, a greenhorn in the industry, and taught the ropes to the young man. (Quite literally, as it turned out)

Each day on the farm taught Jesper valuable lessons about aquaculture and the ways of the world in its natural state. This particular farm site held close to one million salmon. Fifteen pens measured fifty feet by one hundred feet, and every pen held more than fifty-thousand fish. The system floated in the middle of the ocean, secured by huge pontoons, and anchored to the seafloor. And there was a house fixed to the end, with a sixty-foot waterway to the closest island and solid land.

Jesper soon noticed that the Frederick Arm hosted many species of animals. He would encounter them while on duty. From tiny sea creatures clogging the feed nets to seagulls and crows trying to steal the fish food directly from the netted, floating storage sheds. But there was much more that caught his eye during his tenure. Killer Whales, Ravens, Prawns, Crab, and small aquatic mammals were frequently seen on the farm site.

A Cognitive Project

Of all the beautiful experiences Jesper had on the fish farm, one bittersweet story stood out in his mind. It had taken place after his first month working for the company, and at that time, he imagined his experience was common for the environment he worked within. Instead, it would be less common than expected and showed again that nature works in mysterious ways.

Yarley had called the other staff over to pen number two on the north side of the system. He stood back and admired a massive bird, sitting on the guidewire across the pen, staring down at the horde of fresh fare below.

"He's gonna die," Yarley said in his broken English.

It was a gigantic Herron, and its legs were as long as its sleek feathered body. It only took a minute for the farmers to frighten the bird away, and it spanned its wings to a good five feet across before flying off to the trees on the nearby island. Yarley knew it'd be back.

"Why is he going to die, Yarley?" Asked Jesper.

Yarley thought for a moment, still glaring off to the trees in the distance. "He will keep trying to get fish. It will be too hard for him to give up, and he'll die trying."

The workers continued with their duties and laughed internally at Yarley's far-fetched claims. The bird can't reach the fish. If it tried, it would bog down in the water, and its thick, feathered wings would struggle to gain lift, quickly drowning the bird. Jesper thought to himself. *That stunning bird can't be that stupid, indeed.*

The next day the bird had come back, as Yarley had predicted. It sat on the guidewire on pen number two again and stared down at the circling feast below. Yarley walked past the crew and thumbed at the bird calling the seafowl a *shithead*. Somehow, that would become the Herron's affectionate nickname moving forward, and Shithead would come back every day until week's end.

On the final day, it was shift change, and Jesper looked forward to his days off. Just four more hours of work, and he'd be back on the crew boat home for a long week. After their morning cup of coffee and mandatory environmental criteria, the crew made their way out to the pens to feed the fish before passing on their duties.

They noticed it right away. After an entire week of primitive bonding, Shithead floated in pen number two, and his body was lifeless. Yarley was right again. The bird couldn't resist the temptations and tried to capture one of the fish as a reward, but the sea ate him up. They netted the lifeless bird's body from the pen and agreed it must have happened in the night. Yarley took Shithead to the island and buried him under the trees. Jesper reflected on the boat ride home, and he was saddened.

A Cognitive Project

X

The White Pigeon of Hillingdon

The big day had been planned for months, and Carlo would see some notable historic buildings and tributes today. He would be taking the Underground to see the world-famous Trafalgar Square in the heart of London, near the River Thames. That would be his morning, and in the afternoon, he would travel with his family into the London Borough of Hillingdon for supper, where his great aunt resided. It would be a truly marvellous day.

When Carlo arrived at the famous square, history greeted him. The courtyard was direct across from The National Gallery. The square had two large, flower-shaped fountains, and it was a gathering place with numerous benches and trees outlining the area. The crowned achievement at the monument was the one-hundred-sixty-nine-foot Nelson's Column, cornered by four resting black lions. The square commemorates the Battle of Trafalgar that took place in the year 1805.

Surprisingly enough, what Carlo noticed most of all was the pigeons. There were hundreds of them, maybe even thousands. They were a mix of diverse colours, and some walked with a clubbed foot. They all cooed loudly.

It could have been a scene from an Alfred Hitchcock movie, as they were everywhere. Being hand-fed by the tourists and dropping their waste every few seconds seemed to create a madhouse, but people in the square were happy and convinced this was normal behaviour.

Carlo would chase the birds and watch them swarm in packs. Different greys and tans, hues of blue, and even some green adorned the miss-understood birds. They flew overhead and strutted along the pavement, looking for a treat, and Carlo would later admit, he had never seen such a spectacle in his entire life. Once he finished exploring the rest of the square and the numerous historical buildings in the greater London area, he caught the underground back to his family, where they prepared for the trip up the road to the township of Hillingdon.

Carlo and his family departed around three o'clock in the afternoon that same day, and Carlo still pondered how the locals drove their cars in the left lane while steering from the right-hand side of the vehicle. And the roundabouts, they were everywhere, it seemed. But once they had arrived at Carlo's Auntie's house, it was clear that he would remain entertained for the evening, which included a traditional, British meal to tide him over.

His great Aunt lived in an attractive house with an inspiring piece of land. It was the backyard, in particular, that reminded Carlo of an enchanted and lush jungle. The yard would allow Carlo to explore and appreciate the different types of foliage around the garden. And the shrubbery itself was full of bountiful vegetables. From long carrots to shelled peas, squash, pumpkin and chives growing wild, Carlo could see that his Aunt kept up with the garden's maintenance, and it was all finished with wooden walkways and pretty coloured wildflowers.

A cobbled path ran from the back of the house to the rear of the yard, which was easily eighty-five feet deep. Every ten feet would introduce another type of shrub or bush, and there were nasty insects of all kinds.

As Carlo approached the back of the yard, he knew his Aunt would be announcing supper soon, so he decided to turn around and make one more stop back in the garden. Before he did, though, something caught his eye in the thick bush near the rear gate. Carlo took a step closer and could see a white object in the wiry bush. Perhaps it was a plastic bag or some sort of trash, but he needed to know and moved further to the left to see.

To Carlo's surprise, it was a lonely white pigeon. Maybe the most handsome bird he had ever seen. It was solid and pure white, like a glorious dove. Carlo just couldn't recall any white pigeons at the Square earlier. *There weren't any white pigeons at all*, he thought.

He crept a little bit closer, and both sets of eyes met in a tight and expressive gaze. The pigeon didn't have a mark on him. Pure white as the driven snow, and it just sat there on a branch staring back at Carlo. He opened his mouth to speak to the bird, but nothing came out, and the stare down continued. Carlo was afraid to spook the bird and couldn't believe how close he could get to the creature. Why isn't it flying away? He pondered.

There wasn't much time to think about the encounter. Within two long minutes, the white pigeon blinked twice and then fell out of the bush, landing hard at Carlo's feet. It was immediately stiff and had died before it hit the ground, it seemed. *But why?* Carlo asked himself. *What just happened here?* He stared down at the bird, and there was no further movement. It just fell from the bush and died. He had witnessed the last moments of the pigeon's life and couldn't have even imagined such a deep and profound instant. He left the bird where it was and sadly strolled back to the house, defeated and broken.

The multiple pigeons throughout the day had brought Carlo several emotions. From fear to fascination and happiness to sorrow, later on in the day. *It must have had a heart attack*, he imagined. But if nothing else, at least Carlo was able to meet the White Pigeon of Hillingdon and thank it for teaching yet another inevitability of life. Your time is precious and not certain. Love is perceived.

A Cognitive Project

So, tell me, was I able to fool you in the end?

I've just presented you with ten short stories about amazing animal encounters. Of course, you've been given the benefit of knowing that eight of those stories were true, only having different character names. Two of the stories were fictionalized and made up from my imagination. Which two do you think were made up?

Again, this just goes to show you that the information you hear is really up to the individual to believe or not. One needs to consider the source of the information and the credibility of the presenter. Is it a scientific notion or a hypothesis requiring some better explanation? And finally, does the data make sense to you? Can your brain imagine that the information could be accurate, or would you question the facts and dive deeper? I would imagine it would have to do with the situation, but this premise can speak to every single chapter in this specific project.

Whether you believe in ghosts or not, you have made a decision based on your mind's belief. It's the same as our vast universe and our planet Earth. Even religion, where we think we are educated and know the absolute truth. But how much do we honestly know? What is still to be proven as we continue to evolve as a species?

Thanks for playing. The two fictional stories were *Centennial Horror* and *Moose Suicide*.

"The Christian religion is a parody on the worship of the sun, in which they put a man called Christ in the place of the sun, and pay him the adoration originally paid to the sun." - Thomas Paine (1737-1809)

A Cognitive Project

Religion

When I ask you if you believe in God, what is your response? Some of you may say, 'No, I don't believe in God.' Others may already be offended by my asking. The idea of organized religion seems always to be clouded by controversy and painful misunderstanding. I have to wonder why religion is a complex subject to discuss with others. I notice that God-fearing people tend to get easily insulted when challenging their faith. That makes perfect sense when we realize that *some form of religion has caused all major conflicts in Earth's history.*

Before I go further, I want to clarify that I have no intention to test your faith or change your beliefs. If the idea of God brings you comfort, then that's all that matters. But I'll challenge some views that were once very dear to my own heart, and I'll ask some difficult questions, begging for real answers that have yet to be revealed to us. The truth is sometimes difficult to handle.

There are multiple religions on our planet. There have been for thousands of years, and each faith glorifies an entirely different god or deity. I'll focus mainly on *Christianity* in this section, but multiple gods tell me that people want and need to believe in some comfort. Something that they've been taught at an early age and

Religion

passed down from generations before. Believe it or don't believe it, this was the same path that so many followed.

Growing up, my parents had their own beliefs on the subject, but they never pushed me in a specific direction. I discovered religion on my own, and I went through the entire gamete from a young age. For me, the idea of religion made sense because so many others around me were believers in God, and in my case, Jesus Christ.

I can still remember reciting the Lord's Prayer in elementary school. Every weekday, we would start the day by singing Oh Canada and reciting the prayer. It was common for everyone, and at that time, no one even questioned it. And then we all received a copy of *The New Testament*. It was a bright red edition, small and bound. It was a cool little pocketbook that explained the life of Jesus Christ, his miracles, and eternal healing. I felt special just holding the book, to be quite honest.

I read the New Testament from cover to cover. Every word and I tried to retain as much as I could. But it was a challenge at that age. My mind was in plenty of different locations in my teens, and much of the language was foreign to me. I read it, and I believed in the vague content because so many others did, and no one was challenging it. The *Gospel* became reliable to me, but I was already looking to pursue the faith's obscurities.

A Cognitive Project

I became pretty intrigued. I told my parents that I thought of going to a church, and they supported that choice. They bought me a brilliant copy of the Holy Bible, and I started that night with the book of Genesis.

After reading the entire Old Testament, I was more confused than ever. It was a completely different look at biblical times and contained terrific stories, some hard to believe and many devastating destructions on the planet conflicting all humanity. I wanted to understand more, so I joined a local Lutheran church, becoming confirmed soon after. I wanted to go to Heaven. It sounded great.

I took it so seriously that I joined a Sunday school and attended service every week for more than two years. I learned quite a lot during this time, but I had many questions for my Pastor. Some of my questions were greeted with answers that sounded like a fantasy to me, but I kept challenging him to convince me that God existed and Jesus was going to save my soul. He could tell I was frustrated. I prayed to God every night before going to sleep, as I committed myself to Jesus and wanted salvation. Happiness is what I asked from God.

During this time, I re-read the entire bible again. I started with the Old Testament and following it up with the New Testament. This time, I would really dive into it and see how much made sense to me in my mind. By this

Religion

time, I was through high school and about to go out on my own. Rereading the scriptures opened my eyes, and I started to talk to others who questioned their faith as I slowly started to. And then I read all about Atheism.

I left the church, moving from town, and never looked back. I had, and still have, great respect for the idea of religion, but by this time, I was starting to make a conscious choice that would define my arrival into adulthood. I kept my bible close and referenced it often.

I chose to keep my faith a secret for various reasons, even when I was fully engaged. The people in my life who weren't associated with the church didn't know different. It seemed taboo, causing so many arguments and ending loving relationships because varied faiths and religions were veiling the perception of real love.

When I entered my twenties, I began to back away from God. I prayed much less and realized that my life was proceeding, good and bad, regardless of my faith. I started to research at the library and tried to understand what happens to us when we die. It was a daunting task, and at the end of the day, not only was there *no proof that God existed but there was no proof against it either*.

Once I was able to research online, it was evident that no matter how much or how long I searched and read about religion, I wasn't going to be successful in finding

A Cognitive Project

any definitive answers. We just don't know yet for sure, and I've tried to contemplate the subject simply. I've dissected it, trying to recognize what made sense in my head and what never really did, even in the beginning.

The rest of this chapter will contain an opinion from my research. Again, I do not propose that I'm correct in my assumptions, but perhaps it might allow you to look at religion and Christianity in a whole different light.

Heaven and Hell

First, I considered *Heaven* and *Hell*. From day one, I was taught that I would end up in one of these two places when I died. If I surrendered to my god and trusted the assurance of serine infinity from Jesus, I would land in heaven and reunite with my ancestry who passed before me. If I chose not to follow God's word, I would be eternally punished in scorching fire and brimstone beside the Devil in Hell. It scared me to even imagine it at first.

If God forgives everyone, why does Hell exist? If the true believers go to Heaven, why is there no evidence of this magical place? If it exists in the skies, is it near to us or millions of light-years away? The word 'Hell' does not appear in the original Holy Bible, and I mentioned my opinion of what happens to our souls once we die in the paranormal chapter. I don't believe either of these places exists. One place brings us comfort, and the other brings us fear. Fear and hope have been a familiar pattern followed by human beings since the beginning of time. Even the Catholic church has admitted that 'Hell' is a made-up place that scares people into staying close to their congregation. Personally, I don't worry about this place. When I leave this lifetime, I will return anew.

Multiple Gods

The gods that most of us believe in are not the first gods. There have been hundreds of gods throughout time, and each has been glorified, similar to the son, Jesus Christ. *How can so many gods be in charge?*

I wanted to get an idea of the different gods that once existed and those that exist today in various cultures worldwide. One of the pieces of theory that I took pretty seriously was from *Zeitgeist, the movie*. The original chapter on religion had a section that compared gods from around the world. These were gods that existed before the birth of Jesus Christ, and they all seemed to share eerie similarities in regards to their live attributes. The gods noted were *Horus (Egypt – 3000 BC)*, *Attis (Greece -1200 BC)*, *Krishna (India – 900 BC)*, *Dionysus (Greece -500 BC)*, *and Mithra (Persia – 1200 BC)*. They alleged that each of these saviours shared all of the same characteristics. Their lives all seemed to follow a similar pattern from birth to death and even their magnificent afterlife.

Initially, this seemed to blow up religion's whole idea out of the water, but it was hard to imagine that more people didn't know about these similar anomalies. The attributes that these gods shared were as follows.

- All were said to have been born on December 25th.

- Most were born of a virgin.

- They were teachers, and most had twelve disciples.

- They could all perform miracles (Dionysus turned water into wine, and Horus healed the sick and even allegedly walked on water.)

- Some of them were crucified, and all resurrected.

- They all shared names such as the light, the omega, the son, the alpha, and the lamb of God.

It seemed apparent that all of the gods had been personified the same way over multiple generations from the beginning. This started to make sense to me, as it would follow a copycat mentality, passed down through an ancestry trail. But then I realized that Christianity had tricked me. I was led to believe the information I read, but it contained some holes, and I wanted to be accurate.

After some more research, I realized that many of the gods' similar attributes were not entirely accurate. In fact, almost every single god mentioned had at least one feature that was not historically correct. I forced myself to look elsewhere for answers, but I found another part of the Zeitgeist chapter even more prolific.

It would simply suggest that all religion, specifically Christianity, could be an astrological spectacle shared over time and misconstrued over the last two thousand plus years. It was the most believable theory on religion that I'd ever seen, and for once, it was starting to come together. At least in my mind, it certainly did.

I thought of the people during that time. They were living in the Middle East's cruel temperatures with very few luxuries and limited technological know-how. What did these people do to pass the time? They loved and fought as we do, but what did they do to entertain themselves and find some worth during their lives? Their choices were limited, but the answers were always there.

Son of God, or Sun of God?

The Zeitgeist movie makes a moderately poignant argument. When we look up at our sky today, we are still fascinated with the fantastic spectacle above us, and we wonder what could exist in the vastness of space. We have taken it for granted now that we have an influx of information flooding our social media accounts and available to us at the click of the button. When Jesus lived, the skies may have been the most significant part

A Cognitive Project

of their cultural existence. The obscurities would have probably been speculated much differently than today.

We know that as far back as 10,000 BC, history is rich with writings and carvings about the sun. It had been respected and adorned as the saviour of life, saving humanity with its warmth, vision and security, allowing the crops to grow and the predators to flee. Without the sun, people understood that life on the planet would not survive. The sun became the most decorated entity of all time and the most influential object in the sky. These early ancestors knew much more about the skies than the typical human being does now. And that's a fact.

They also studied the stars in the sky and followed their patterns over time, and they would survey them over long time periods. They would catalogue the exact movements, and eventually, the most prominent clusters would be named the constellations. These are the same constellations that astronomers and we follow today.

One of the oldest conceptual images in human history is the cross of the zodiac. It reflects the eternal sun as it passes its way, figuratively, through the twelve major constellations throughout the year. It also depicts the twelve months of the year, the four seasons, and the solstices and equinoxes. Early civilizations who studied the skies would personify the twelve constellations as figures or animals. They would create elaborate myths about their movements with the sun. With its warmth and life-saving assets, the sun would have been personified as an unseen representative of the almighty creator. It was coined as the *Sun of God*. The saviour of humankind, the light of the world and proof that they weren't alone.

Jesus Christ was said to be born on December 25th. Yet, there is no record of this date in the Holy Bible. He was born of a *virgin* in a manger which we need to understand is not possible. Female pregnancy has, and always will be, a chemical reaction in which the female egg needs to be fertilized by the male's sperm. This has always been the case, and I can't possibly believe that it happened at that time with the birth of Jesus Christ. It does, however, keep relatively consistent with other solar messiahs and their similarly reported life attributes. In fact, the stars explain quite a lot of the bible's content.

The story is that Jesus was a child teacher at twelve years old and baptized at thirty. He was followed by twelve disciples and performed miracles like healing the sick, raising the dead and walking on water. After being betrayed by his disciple, Judas, he was crucified on the cross and was placed in a tomb. After three days, he resurrected and ascended into Heaven. The argument is that this entire birth sequence appears to be primarily astrological. Please, let me explain what I mean by that.

A Cognitive Project

Jesus' birth was announced by a *star in the east* which *three kings* followed to locate and adorn the new saviour. The star in the east would be the brightest in the night sky, Sirius. This star aligns with the three brightest stars in Orion's Belt on December 24th. The three stars in Orion's Belt are called today what they were called in ancient times, *The Three Kings*. The Three Kings and Sirius all point to the place of the sunrise on December 25th. This would be why the Three Kings follow the star in the east to locate the sunrise or the sun's birth. God's Sun, or the *Sun of God*. But the astrological similarities don't stop there and permit us to question more about what ancient civilizations thoroughly observed.

Another natural phenomenon will occur every year around December 25th or the winter solstice. From the summer solstice to the winter solstice, civilizations knew that the days became colder and shorter. From the Northern hemisphere perspective, the sun appears to move south and become smaller and scarcer. The shortness of the days would symbolize the concept of death to the ancient populations. To them, it was the death of the sun as crops withered, and the cold arrived.

The sun makes it to the lowest point in the sky on December 22nd. Perceivably, the sun stops moving south for a total of three days. During this three-day hiatus, the sun resides in the Crux Constellation vicinity, also known as the *Southern Cross*, by ancient civilizations. After this, on December 25th. The sun moves one degree, this time to the north. This foreshadowed the longer days, warmth, and the celebration of Spring and grand survival. They interpreted this as *The Sun died on the cross, was dead for three days, only to be resurrected or born again.* It is why Jesus and other solar Messiahs share the same birth attributes on the 25th of December and resurrection after three days. The stars told them the story, and we have misunderstood since its infancy.

These tales were transferred into written scripture and compiled into a series of books we know as the bible. Is it possible that everything we know about Jesus Christ is what they translated from the stars? Unfortunately, the Christian Cross isn't of Christian origin at all. It's actually a pagan symbol of the zodiac sign, and generations have been duped into thinking this was a symbol of torture and death. We must remember that the only reason we know the fate of Jesus is because one book has told us so. Yes, Jesus was a real man, and he didn't have white skin, but we also know that Santa Claus was a real man. He gave gifts to the needy children and brought happiness. We know the stories of Kris Kringle, sliding down chimneys and delivering presents to all the good boys and girls around the world. But then we were able to understand that an old, portly man would never be able to fly with magical reindeer, and the tales of Santa Clause became a folk story, widely accepted by most children today. For me, though, I don't understand why we didn't connect the same cognitive reasoning when it came to the stories in the bible. And some of them are much harder to believe than those of St. Nick.

The Bible says it to be true...

As a writer, I can recognize fiction. My head is full of it every day. When I re-read the bible, some of the stories lacked a sense of reality that we have recognized from birth. It's an actual reality that just won't allow things to transpire how they were depicted in the great book. Here are some examples. You may elect to agree or disagree.

Jesus walked on water

Did a living man categorically walk on water, or was this translated wrong from the very beginning? Perhaps someone witnessed Jesus crossing a grassy path above a water source, which is how it was perceived. Maybe he had walked through a shallow puddle, and his grandeur provoked a magical depiction of the event. There were most certainly mind intoxicants and alcohol that clouded perception at times, and it would have been fascinating to depict someone as a great assistant to God while alive on Earth. *If an occurrence hasn't transpired before or since then, it just can't be validated as the truth. But how quickly I forget.* Horus walked on water also. So, this has happened twice? Maybe it's been a tale woven over time to verify both of the deities? *This is false information.*

Noah's Unbelievable Ark

This story has intrigued and bothered me for a long time now. It's an incredible tale, but the more you think about it, the easier it is to see that this was an impossible task. *An amazing man gathered a male and female of every species on Earth and loaded them upon a massive ark that he built himself to save them and all of humanity from the great flood.* Once again, science makes this a little bit tricky for us to imagine as reality.

I can't dispute the fact that Noah may have built himself a glorious ship, but let's honestly look at the facts. First of all, Noah would have collected (ready for this?) 70,000 animals. There were approximately 35,000 land animal species, and he needed one of each sex for success. Science has proven that an ark, large enough to carry every single animal, could indeed float, but how big would this vessel need to be? If you consider the species alive during that biblical time, they would have been surrounded by similar creatures that we see today. We must also consider the obvious question which fictionalizes this story almost immediately, and we can't just ignore it because it wouldn't be credible even now.

A Cognitive Project

How was Noah able to gather these animals? How was he to ensure that he collected one of each sex, and how did he get them to follow him to the magnificent ark? There were many different species around the world, and far away from Noah's location. How did those animals come and board, two by two, and most importantly, how were they fed once the great flood commenced? I would imagine they would have been quite hungry and needing fresh water. The freshwater required to keep these animals alive would have required a deep hold of its own. I've often wondered how Noah could control some species' predatory instinct and can't even imagine the number of cages needed to stow the birds, snakes, rodents, and insects. How did they all eat?

Many will agree that the account of Noah's Ark was indeed fictional in the bible, but if this particular story was a myth, is it too hard to believe that other parts of the bible are as well? In case you're wondering, the Ark, in this case, would have needed to be at least nine stories high, with a length of three football fields and a width of one football field. It would have been similar to our largest cruise ships sailing today, and it would have been the most impressive floating achievement ever built.

The fact is, Noah and his Ark were lifted by the ancient writing *The Epic of Gilgamesh*, written in 2600 BC. The tale speaks about a great flood, commanded by

God, an Ark which would save animals upon it, and even the release and return of a white dove to scout for land. The references of great floods are well documented over time in many historical references, and it can't be denied.

The Story of Moses

The bible will convince you that some of the stories are unique and true to the modern belief and following. Many tales within the bible have been derived from ancient sources and reconstructed. The story of Moses in the Old Testament is a perfect example of this.

It was said that once Moses was born, he was put into a reed basket and set adrift in a river. This was to avoid infanticide. He was rescued by a daughter of royalty and raised as a prince. But this story has some history. The tale itself was plagiarized from the myth of *Sargon of Akkad*. (2,250 BC) Sargon was placed in a basket at birth and sent down a river to avoid infanticide, later rescued by a royal midwife. Remember, this would have taken place 2,250 years before the birth of Jesus Christ.

Moses was looked at as the lawgiver. The giver of the ten commandments. The idea of these commanding laws passed down by God to a prophet from a mountain top is similar to old motifs. Moses was just another lawgiver in a long line throughout history. This is recognized by different religious sects and can add to the evidence of a fictional scripture. Even the mighty ten commandments themselves came directly from the *Egyptian Book of the Dead*. The truth is that the Christian ideology may simply result from the ancient Egyptian philosophies. The crazy similarities are countless. It begins with the virgin birth, the adoration, resurrection, baptism, final judgement, the holy communion, Passover, Easter, Christmas, circumcision, afterlife, crucifixion, saviours, and even the great flood. All were referenced from ancient Egyptian scripture and bent into a brand-new story about a man sharing the same attributes and saving the world. When actually, the world has always been saved by the Sun. The *Sun of God* as it should be known.

Joseph and Jesus

When we look at Joseph in the Old Testament and Jesus Christ in the New Testament, we face undeniable evidence of many fictional accounts and different misinterpretations. By thinking for yourself, you can easily see the holes in Christianity and all religions.

Joseph was just a prototype for Jesus. Joseph had a miracle birth like Jesus. Joseph was one of twelve brothers. Jesus had twelve disciples. Joseph was sold for twenty pieces of silver; Jesus was sold for thirty pieces of silver. Brother *Judah* suggests the sale of Joseph, and disciple *Judas* suggests the sale of Jesus. Both men began their work at the age of thirty. The likenesses to both men actually go on and on. Many historians that were alive during biblical times never mention Jesus in their transcripts. A man of God who heals the sick and performs miracles, but he's not declared in the official records? We may need to think about that for a moment.

The Ages

Today, we live in the *Age of Pisces*. This is why Jesus is depicted in the Bible, relating to *fish* many times. Surely, you've seen the *Jesus Fish* on the rear bumpers of vehicles. The term 'Age' is used numerous times in the bible, which is also purely astrological. An Age is a period of 2,150 years, and long before Jesus, between the years of 4,300 BC and 2150 BC, we were in the *Age of Taurus, the Bull*. Between the years of 2150 BC and 1 AD, we were in the *Age of Aries, the Ram*. And in the year 2150, we will enter into the new Age. It will be the *Age of Aquarius,* the Water Bearer who carries a pitcher.

There are numerous writings in the bible about the Ages. It is scribed as depicting three distinct Ages while foreshadowing a fourth. The Old Testament states that when Moses descends Mount Sinai with the historic Ten Commandments, he is quite upset that the Israelites are worshiping a golden bull calf. He shatters the tablets and ordered his people to kill each other to purify their souls.

A Cognitive Project

The reality is that Moses represented the new *Age of Aries*, and it was written that he ordered chaos because his people were adorning a false God. The bull calf represented the *Age of Taurus*, and as it was said, everyone must shed the old Age. One of the most renowned scriptures in the New Testament comes from the book of Luke when Jesus is asked by his disciples where the next Passover will be once he is gone. This was his response in the third book of the New Testament.

"Behold, when ye are entered into the city, there shall a man meet you bearing a pitcher of water... follow him into the house where he entereth in." -Luke 22:10

The man bearing the pitcher of water is Aquarius. He represents the *Age after Pisces*, and when God's Sun leaves the Age of Pisces (Jesus), it will move into the *Age of Aquarius*, as Aquarius follows Pisces in the precession of the equinoxes. All Jesus is saying in this scripture is after the Age of Pisces comes Aquarius.

Over time this would mean that civilization would start praying to an entirely new and different god. The truth is, this will never happen unless the planet faces a mass human extinction event. The book of Revelation may well be foreshadowing this event; however, when we look at the history of the Earth and its destructive path from nature, it would be easy to predict this happening at some point. It would seem to me that Christianity's whole concept has been duplicated and miss-translated over time. Christianity may stem from a completely different region globally, and there's even some concrete sustainable proof to back it all up. It would be evidence that can't be ignored or easily dismissed if we tried.

There is solid evidence that Christianity may have been plagiarized from the Egyptian Sun God, *Horus*, who shares many similar characteristics to that of Jesus Christ. There are inscriptions on the Temple of Luxor walls in Egypt, which were inscribed more than 3,500 years ago. That would have been fifteen centuries before Christianity, but the similarities to Jesus Christ are pretty staggering. The stone walls depict the annunciation, the immaculate conception, the Holy Ghost impregnating the virgin, Isis, and then the virgin birth and adoration. This is the precise same way that the birth sequence of Jesus Christ is described in the pages of the Holy Bible.

Other Modern Gods

Probably the thing that bothers me most about religion is the belief in multiple divinities. It makes absolutely no sense to me how a Christian can say that other gods don't exist, and this goes for every other religion not believing in the Christian God, Jesus Christ. If different faiths are bestowed on numerous societies, it may just bring them a sense of security. I can honestly understand how believing in a god can be comforting, allowing us to feel safe and have hope after our deaths. What I can't understand is why we have to fight and argue about it. We can believe in something and know that in reality, it might not be there. In the end, if people want to believe in a god, they should be respected for their beliefs, and it has to work both ways. But we also have to calculate the chances of these modern gods, or any other gods may have never existed. Have faith in what makes you comfortable, but consider our reality.

One of the most compelling opinions and statements about religion comes from Ricky Gervais, who appeared on the Stephen Colbert show in 2017. This makes sense.

"If we take something like any fiction or any holy book and destroyed it, in a thousand years' time, that wouldn't come back just as it was. Where if we took every science book, and every fact and destroyed them all, in a thousand years they would all be back because all the same tests would be the same result."   - Ricky Gervais

And finally, I can greatly relate to the ending of the Zeitgeist opinion, where the narrator sums up everything I've mentioned in this chapter. It's not meant to hurt any feelings, but the following seems to be closer to the truth than what we've been taught. We all deserve the facts.

Religion

"Christianity, along with all other theistic belief systems, is the fraud of the Age. It serves to detach the species from the natural world and likewise each other. It supports blind submission to authority. It reduces human responsibility to the effect that God controls everything, and in turn, awful crimes can be justified in the name of the divine pursuit. And most importantly, it empowers those who know the truth but use the myth to manipulate and control societies. The religious myth is the most powerful device ever created by man and serves as the phycological soil upon which other myths can flourish."

- Zeitgeist

Some of you may agree with my opinions on this subject, and others will assuredly disagree. Regardless of your beliefs and your faith, we need to all respect each other's unique views. Whether you agree with religion or not, the truth is that we don't have constructive proof, either way. All we can do is define our status as a society and do our best to scientifically prove some of the most demanding theories existing in today's civilization. In Christianity's profound case, the entire belief system could have been plagiarized from the historical past and could very well be known as *The Greatest Story Ever Told to Mankind.* In case you're wondering, I believe in *nature.* Mother Nature is my God, and the universe will continue to be my home, even after my impending death.

A Cognitive Project

Everything is connected. From the irritating tsetse fly to the flamboyant butterfly who started life as an ugly caterpillar. Even the acorn that brings life to the mighty Oak or a violent tropical storm cleaning the air and creating a fresh landscape for rebirth. It's all connected.

Instead of viewing our existence through the eyes of an unproven god, maybe we can appreciate the *natural* wonder around us. It surrounds us daily and orchestrates our motivation. If we plant a seed and tend to it properly, it will grow. It grows because of what we have, not because of what we've been told we have. Have faith in life, and cherish the opportunity to live it to the fullest.

I asked a friend once, "Why do you believe in God?"

He replied, "Years back, my daughter had sustained a major head injury. I rushed her to the hospital, and the initial news wasn't good. I sat by myself in the waiting room, and *I prayed to God, over and over again,* asking if she could be spared by Jesus and continue living her life. Thankfully, she slowly improved and eventually, she fully recovered. That's why I believe in God."

I nodded my head and felt empathy for him and his daughter. But I would often wonder how many parents had prayed to God when their child was sick, and they *didn't survive*? Perhaps Heaven isn't a real *place*. Maybe it's a *space* in our *universe*, offering us second chances.

"The universe had to fall apart into dust first to become its majestic, incredible, infinite self. What makes you think this breaking, this trauma, this destruction, won't be the making of a more powerful you too?" - Nikita Gill

A Cognitive Project

The Universe

Where does one start? Just like the universe, there seems to be no beginning and no end for that matter. While researching this particular chapter, I faced the most controversial and ambiguous theories I've ever seen. If I found something that captivated me, I soon found another article that disproved it. And then I would find something else that disproved that one. I realized that I would have to base my opinion on what made sense to me, and when it comes to our universe, scientists and astronomers are only scratching the surface of what the cosmos has to offer us. And the progress changes daily.

Most of us learned in school about the *nine* planets in our solar system. We learned about the sun and the procession of the planets around this glorious object. We knew we had a moon, and other planets had multiple moons. The size of Jupiter would shock us, and Saturn's rings amazed us. The Earth was our place of comfort.

After that, we really didn't know too much. We knew what NASA was telling us, and the truth was, we didn't even have a clear understanding of our own planet. It was easy for us to believe human accomplishments in space because it was such a mammoth task for us. We had to trust the evidence told to us because it's all we had.

And then Pluto wasn't a planet anymore...

Our solar system now only has eight 'planets' that orbit our sun. I have to admit, when I first heard this, I was floored. I had known, my whole life, about the ninth planet, Pluto, but now we were to disregard it altogether.

It was somehow decided in August of 2006 when the *International Astronomical Union (IAU)* downgraded Pluto's status to a 'Dwarf Planet.' The IAU concluded that Pluto only met two of the three primary criteria to be classified as a planet. So, although it was orbiting our sun and contained a sufficient mass to be defined as a planet, it lacked the ability to *'clear the neighbourhood around its orbit.'* Essentially what this means is Pluto had become 'gravitationally dominant,' meaning that it had no gravitational influence in its vicinity in space. So, Pluto was soon forgotten, as we all accepted this to be a fact that can't be disputed. I won't deny this; it's just not worth it, so now we accept Neptune as the furthest satellite that orbits our sun in the solar system. I can't help but think of Pluto and how pissed off it must be about this. But seriously, this is a highly confusing piece of our interstellar history because we know that this satellite exists. Still, it isn't allowed to join the regal line of planets any longer. The question would be, if a credible source told you another planet was discovered in our solar system, would you believe them?

A Cognitive Project

We Are Not Alone

As mentioned in the previous chapter, people have been looking up at the stars for thousands of years. The sky is wondrous at night and offers a picture show that television can't replicate in the right conditions. But few seem to understand just what they're looking at when viewing the stars above. When we put our sights into perspective, we can easily digest our existence's true insignificance relating to the bigger picture. And the picture is massive—infinity big, as a matter of fact.

Each prick of light we can see in the night sky is one of only a few different things. They are planets, moons, constellations, satellites, galaxies and suns. *That's right; I said suns plural.* We know that our sun is a star, so each star you see in the sky is a sun. Perhaps some are bigger than our sun and many more light-years away, or some may be nearing the end of their lives, ready to perish within their galaxy and cause a new beginning over time.

What's essential for us to understand is that each of these stars or suns probably has rocks orbiting them as our sun does. Outer planets that may be similar to the planets in our solar system, or perhaps they could consist of elements we don't even know exist yet. The point of this chapter will allow you to see just how big these objects are, as it relates to time and speed. It can be pretty mind-boggling but fascinating at the same time. If nothing else, it will enable us to continue educating ourselves with the mysteries of the vast universe. It's the same universe that we call home, and we're not alone.

Suppose we realize the space and distance between the planets in our solar system. In that case, we can learn to appreciate just how massive the universe is and the possible chances of extra-terrestrial lifeforms existing within it. I would imagine there are many millions of un-inhabitable planets orbing around their stars. At least they would be lifeless as it pertains to our understanding of life. Any planet would need to share some pretty impressive characteristics with our Earth for life to flourish and evolve. Without these similar attributes, life as we know it would simply fail to exist.

We have first to consider the lifecycle of the planet and that of its sun as well. Our sun is about halfway through its lifespan, but other stars may be new and young or ready to die in an explosion. The same would go for the planet too. When was it moulded? Which astrological phase could it be going through at that particular time? And then we have to imagine the proximity to its sun. This is vital, as we have learned from our minuscule solar system. Without this proper proximity, the planet would be too cold or too hot to sustain life, and it couldn't be a gaseous world either.

A Cognitive Project

Venus is much too hot, and Mars is far too cold for humans to sustain their populations. The Earth just so happens to be in that sweet spot. The perfect proximity from our sun and a breeding ground for life and success. But just as there are millions of rocks orbiting their suns, outside of this proximity zone, there are many millions more that would sit in the same sweet spot as Earth does.

What a remarkable deliberation it is to ponder the possibilities in the cosmos. If the same elements or the building blocks of life exist, and the planet has an atmosphere protecting it from the cruelty of space, it would have water and support the most basic forms of life. It would seem to be precisely how our existence progressed over millions and millions of years. This evolution could evolve in many different forms. Depending on that planet's weather and meteorological events, it's possible that certain lifeforms could have surpassed what we've been able to achieve thus far.

What if...?

What if one of those tiny pinpricks of light was a star *twice the size* of our sun? Many more light-years away from Earth. Now imagine a planet, in this case, the size of Jupiter or about the *size of 1,300 Earths*. This colossal planet might just sit in this pro-life proximity, and let's say for the sake of argument that this planet and its sun are generally young celestial objects. If this planet contained the building blocks of life, an atmosphere, and life-generating freshwater, there could be many thousands of different species there. They could be as simple as our amoeba and others whose intelligence may far surpass our own. We are just another species in a universe full of life. This seems crystal clear to me.

Perhaps this alien world contains humanoid creatures that have evolved much longer than we have here on Earth. And just maybe this civilization wasn't created from greed and organized religion. This species could be friendly and have no desire for bloodshed. Perhaps they have spent their entire existence working together for the greater cause of their planet and created technologies that we can only imagine. Strength in numbers for sure.

Remember, if the planet was the size of Jupiter, it could easily sustain (under Earth's conditions) upwards of 900-billion beings. Can you imagine if this existence was civilized, past our standards, and all worked together? A planet like this wouldn't need to worry about the Earth, even if they knew we existed. To them, we would be an insignificant lifeform who has far too much to learn still. If they were like us, they would be doomed.

Of course, if these were Earth's conditions, this planet would suffer the same conservation issues and even mass extinction events throughout its history. Like on Earth, life would undoubtedly find a way to survive. *Just like a tiny seed implanted in soil and fed some freshwater, life will always find a way to endure.* This planet could be one of the billions that exist through the known universe.

This particular intelligent species would most likely communicate differently than we do. They wouldn't use our alphabet, and their languages would sound much different than we can recognize here, back at home. The potential is truly endless, depending on their evolution.

For me, the extra-terrestrial reports I've researched are spotty at best. Some are clearly faked, and others beg an explanation. These Unidentified Flying Objects are pretty fascinating, but I would think this to be quite a rudimentary way of travel for an existence with obvious technological intellect that far surpasses our own. We have tiredly studied teleportation and time travel. I would imagine that the most intelligent species in our universe wouldn't use something as simple as a flying ship to get around, but that's just my meek opinion.

That planet would exist outside of our galaxy. We are spending billions of dollars to investigate Mars, and some of the photos and videos are mind-blowing. It would seem there is no life on Mars right now. Still, it certainly looks like there may have been at some time.

Maybe, hundreds of thousands of years ago, there may have been significant lifeforms on Mars. Still, outside of this option, it would be infinitely difficult for life, as we know it, to exist on any other planet in the Milky Way Galaxy. It's just too harsh, and right now, our technology won't help us. That would be the end goal for us, though.

We are blessed to be in the right proximity to the sun. I'm sure you've realized from the last chapter; I don't believe we were put here by creation. The reason we are here is that this rock we live on can sustain life. And our existence, in my opinion, didn't start with Adam and Eve. The story is far too complex to be accurate, and we can completely understand how life actually begins and the unfortunate way it ceases to exist at times. We've been through some actual hell here on Earth, and we will also feel the wrath of the cosmos someday. But we will return once again, picking up where we left off.

Astronomers know very little about the universe. We've only scratched the surface in reality. We've been able to send an unmanned spacecraft to observe each planet in our solar system, and powerful telescopes can peer deep into the depths of outer space. They can monitor billions of independent constellations, galaxies, nebulas, planets, moons, and even the elusive *Black Hole*. What we've photographed and documented, however, is a tiny square of area. The vastness of space extends to points that we have yet to discover. We're not even close yet, but technology is flourishing at an astounding pace, and we will see significant progress.

Could there be alternate dimensions or multiple doors to other universes out there? That's way over my head, but I think it's fair to say that the possibility is somewhat likely. After a ton of research, I kept coming across pages that were even arguing the fact that we've never sent a man into outer space. From *alleged NASA lies* to the conspiracy about the *moon landings*, some have even proposed that we cannot leave Earth's outer atmosphere. Just when I thought I could develop an honest opinion, there seemed to be more to consider, and I needed to dig further into other views that existed out there.

I've watched a video of actual astronaut interviews. The newer version has the astronauts speaking about the stars and how many there are. Even in the middle of the day, the stars were everywhere in great abundance. But the interview that I watched from the 1960s featured two astronauts who swore there were no stars to be seen in space. One of them couldn't recollect seeing even one, as his partner looked at him, nervously and the camera rolled. Once again, there's some proof of a contradiction. Someone is lying to us, and the motivation for the cover-up is unclear. Video doesn't lie, and some are most likely valid. It is concrete evidence, and it can't be erased.

Some of the many truthers out there have posted very compelling video evidence of NASA's many cover-ups. One stimulating argument is the existence of CGI. Many will claim that all the video we see from space is simply computerized right here on Earth with actors in space simulators. We know that astronauts train in water to limit gravity and allow them to experience what space feels like, but the videos and articles presented more.

Air bubbles. In space? Well, you wouldn't think this is possible, yet many taped spacewalks seem to show these air bubbles leaving the astronaut's helmet and floating away. But I have no idea if those videos have been photo-shopped or tampered with. Multiple other sources show more significant space issues that NASA has neglected to report to us for several years.

There are claims of CGI movement in shuttle or space station video to simulate zero gravity. Some of the items that astronauts interact with don't always line up to reality. There are fade-outs and phony mishandling.

Even the view of Earth from space is under scrutiny. Many are saying that the planet has been photoshopped when shown from space. I'm no expert, but pros can raise or decrease certain levels in the photograph to show that the Earth has been added after the fact. This goes against everything I've ever believed about outer space.

A Cognitive Project

It could simply be some false information, but we must question it all. As you'll see later, the Earth is incredible.

There could also be a NASA cover-up regarding life from other planets. An agreement that could benefit most. Now they have admitted to testing on a crashed alien ship. Like every other subject in this book, there are many different opinions on the truth. I prefer to leave it up to the scientists, but one thing is for sure. It's a challenge to find agreeance when it comes to anything. I will admit that no matter what NASA might be hiding, we would know very little about the universe without them and the countless professional and amateur astronomers globally. What we're told is not what we need to worry about. We shouldn't let it control our lives, but the existing realism within our space is rather deceitful and surreal to us at times, and we want to know.

We needn't worry about our sun dying. It still has about 4.5 billion years of life left in it. Of course, when this happens, the solar flare will incinerate all of the planets in the solar system. But the multiple scars on the planets and moons between the asteroid belt tell a historical tale of bombardment, which includes our Earth on many occasions. We are not safe from space threats.

Our moon looks like 'Swiss Cheese' because of the several meteor impacts in its history. We're able to see the evidence here on Earth too. Some of these craters have been recognized as memories of when Earth went through some dark and treacherous times. Most of us agree that a massive asteroid was responsible for the demise of the dinosaurs. This would make sense if we could imagine the ultimate destruction a giant rock propelling to Earth would bestow on our floating planet. These events are unstoppable and bound to happen again in time. Time, in this case, is classified in hundreds of thousands of years, but the clock doesn't stop, and none of us know when the time will come again. At least now, we will have some warning and a chance to say goodbye to the ones we love, which in itself is a blessing for all.

Beware; the shifting poles

Swamping the internet right now, if you follow the astronomer pages, is the warning about our poles. 'Flipping Polarity' or the reversal of the Earth's poles seem to have fallen into a reversal pattern of 200,000 to 300,000 years. Sometimes the poles try and reverse but snap back unsuccessfully. Such an event took place around 40,000 years ago, and scientists believe that this may have been the dismal end of the Neanderthal race. The total shift of poles has not occurred for 780,000 years now, and we are significantly overdue. The planet's magnetic field is already shifting, convincing scientists that a pole reversal is entirely probable.

A Cognitive Project

The Earth's magnetic field shields the Earth from dangerous solar and cosmic rays. Radiation upon the planet would significantly increase. This would cause entire species to go extinct. Electric grids will fail and lead to worldwide blackouts. The poles' flipping will only increase the number of natural disasters that the planet will have to endure. Seismic movement, volcanic activity, and even our oceans will be highly active.

Enough about the gloom and doom of 'what could happen.' Humans only have a maximum of around one hundred years to learn in this life. There will always be negativity to consider, but there is also a wonderous array of beauty in our cosmos. And sometimes, just to lie back on a clear, cool autumn night and stare at the stars above is all we need in order to feel worthy. To be fully content and appreciative of our one opportunity. We will continue to make wishes on the falling stars until the end of time. (which are not all stars, by the way.) The death of a star guarantees the birth of another wonder. If only we could be a fly on the wall and watch it take place.

Our universe shares secrets. Secrets that educate us and allow us to set goals for our very evolution as a species. Yes, it is a fast-moving, dark void that contains dangers, but to view it from Earth and understand that we're only a mere grain of sand in space gives us hope. It's the void that contains the wonders of our existence.

But what exactly am I referring to when I relate to the universe as *wonderful*? The size of space alone is hard to imagine, but do we all honestly know how big some objects are? Here's a quick and somewhat basic list of some comparable data. And remember, this is only what we know. The unknown is still a mystery for now.

A little comparison on a gargantuan space.

Here's what we know, which isn't a whole lot. Well, okay, this isn't *all we know*. But these are some enormous examples of what I'm talking about, from planets, stars, moons, galaxies, constellations, nebulas, chemical reactions, and cross-sections of outer space.

- To us, the Earth is mammoth. Men and women have travelled around our planet, and many more only wish they could. The *Earth itself is a mere 13,000 km in diameter*. Our planet is an astronomical, *148 million km from the sun* that keeps us all alive and offers warmth. As of now, the Earth is the only planet to sustain life.

- Our smallest planet and the nearest planet to the sun, *Mercury, is only 4,900 km in diameter* and orbits the sun every *88 days*. Mercury is a mere *66 million km away from the blazing star*. We would incinerate immediately.

- *Earth's moon* is similar in size to that of Mercury, with a *diameter of 3,500 km*. This interstellar neighbour gives

A Cognitive Project

us protection and is responsible for much of the natural phenomenon on the planet. Even the moon shares debate.

- *Saturn* is second, only to Jupiter in planetary size within our Solar System. Its glorious rings, composed of boulders and dust, span a tremendous *120,000 km in diameter*. Being the seventh planet from the sun, its warmth is almost non-existent, nearly *1.5 billion km away*. Think of all the stars in the sky. Our sun is the closest star to us, and it shelters millions of miles in area.

- The *sun* itself is a monstrous, *1.4 million km in diameter*. That's nearly *108 Earths*, side by side. Our star is around *4.6 billion years old* and doesn't have enough mass to go supernova. But it will swell into a *Red Giant in another four to five billion years* from now, taking out everything between it and Neptune in a spectacular way.

- The next closest star to the Earth is the star *Proxima Centauri*. As a simple comparison, it's *40.2 Trillion km away* from us. That's the second-closest star, and again, when you look up at the sky, how many do you see? I think you're starting to get the idea here...

The funny thing is that these are just small examples of the size within our universe. There are tangible objects such as the now-famous *VY Canis Majoris. A star with a diameter of 2 billion km*. Can you imagine the planetary objects that might be orbiting around it? With such a huge perimeter, I could see a possibility of more than one planet sharing the same orbit, thousands of kilometres away from one another. The size and real-time needed to navigate these outer areas make them challenging to study, but we continue improving our technology. But what if I told you that space as we know it doesn't exist, and we've never even been there yet? Hear me out here.

It's not necessarily my opinion, but here's what some people are arguing over. We've been unable to leave Earth's outer astrosphere. Some Astro-physicists have recently suggested that the furthest region of our atmosphere, or the *Exosphere*, is even larger than first thought. The Exosphere is the final layer between us and outer space. Now it's been extended to *630,000 km above sea level*. That's even further away than our moon. So theoretically, the moon is actually still well within our atmosphere. The satellites and international space station are situated much lower in the Thermosphere. So basically, with this new theory, humankind has never been to space if indeed space begins once we're through our dense atmosphere and not a mile lower than that.

Will we ever experience it?

Well, probably not in my lifetime, but the technology is flourishing, and it appears as if Elon Musk, along with NASA, is experimenting with some real mind-blowing advancements, which will undoubtedly revolutionize space travel as we know, taking people into the cosmos.

The goal, at the moment, is to build settlements on Mars, but if we can develop a safe form of human travel, I would imagine that the possibilities would be endless. But this begs the question. What is the absolute truth when it comes to our achievements thus far? *Have we really put men on the moon?* Well, we'll save that for another project, but just maybe the conspiracy theorists shouldn't be as wildly scrutinized as they have been.

Did you know?

- The universe is ancient. If you believe in the 'Big Bang Theory,' you realize that the cosmos are around 13.7 billion years old. (Give or take 130 million years.)

- The Universe is flat. The Theory of Relativity tells us the universe is rather open, closed or flat. Astrophysicists believe although the cosmos are flat, planets are round.

- The universe is getting bigger every day. It was Astronomer Edwin Hubble who discovered that the universe is not static and is categorically expanding. Where is it going, and will it ever stop or backtrack?

- It is possible that multiple universes may exist from parallel spaces to perplexing black holes. This would suggest that outer space and time may have expanded at

The Universe

different rates in different places. Other universes could mean separate physics and commanding laws within.

- Venus is the only planet in our solar system that rotates backwards on its axis. *Things that make you go, hmmm.*

- There could be as many as three-sextillion stars in the universe. That's a three with twenty-three zeros behind it. That's even more than all of the grains of salt on Earth.

- Observable matter like stars and planets only make up five percent of the universe. The remaining ninety-five percent is made up of dark matter. It means that we still don't know about ninety-five percent of the universe.

- The Hubble telescope will allow us to look back billions of years into the past. It can produce photos showing thousands of young galaxies and acts as a portal back in time. Even light can take billions of years to reach our sight. Some stars that we see in the sky may have already died. It changes our perception of time.

- Our sun is actually orbiting around the center of our galaxy. Where it takes the Earth three-hundred and sixty-five days to orbit the sun, it takes an astounding 225 million years for the sun to complete a circuit of the galaxy. The last time the sun was in its current position, dinosaurs ruled the Earth on the Pangaea continent. And we all know what happened to those monstrous beasts.

- Mars claims the largest mountain in our solar system. It's called Olympus Mons, and it reaches twenty-six kilometres above the Martian planet. That makes it three times the height of Mount Everest. This shield volcanic mountain is six hundred kilometres across.

- Voyager One, in 2013, became the first human-made object to leave the solar system. It's currently 124.34 Astronomical Units away from Earth. That means it's roughly 1.15581251 x 1010 miles away from us now.

- There are an estimated 400 billion stars in our Galaxy. Like our own star, these all have planets orbiting around them. As many as 500 million or more are known.

Our Solar System

Mercury: A rocky planet, *58 million km.* from the sun. The temperature at a high is *427 degrees Celsius,* and *it has no moons. Mercury's day lasts 59 Earth days.*

Venus: At *462 degrees Celsiu*s, Venus is our hottest planet. It orbits the sun from *108 million km.* away and is considered a sister planet to Earth with similar composition, but it is far too hot for water to exist. *It has no moons,* and a day on Venus would be *225 Earth days.* Venus is the only planet in our system to spin backwards upon its axis, meaning the sun rises in the west and sets in the east. It is often the brightest object in the sky.

The Universe

Earth: Our home is about *150 million km.* from the sun. Our day is slightly over *24 hours*, and we are indeed a rocky planet. Earth has one moon, and the average temperature is *14 degrees Celsius*. Water covers 70% of the Earth's surface, and it's the only planet we know of that can support life. A suggested diamond in the rough.

Mars: *228 million km. from the sun*, Mars is also known as the 'Red Planet.' This rocky planet is the most similar to Earth but has an average *temperature of -63 degrees Celsius*, which frequently fluctuates. A day on Mars is *24 hours and 37 minutes,* and it has *two small moons*.

Jupiter: It's 317 times larger than Earth and *a day lasts 9.8 Earth hours*. Jupiter is a gassy giant and is about *778 million km. from the sun*. Known to have as many as *67 moons*, the *average temperature is -148 degrees Celsius*.

Saturn: At *1.4 billion km. from the sun*, Saturn contains unique rings made up of small boulders and rocks. It's a gas planet with an average *temperature of -178 degrees Celsius*. Saturn has 53 known moons, with nine more moons awaiting confirmation and a *day lasts 10.7 hours*.

Uranus: A gas or ice giant, Uranus is *2.9 billion km. from the sun*. It reaches a chilly *-216 degrees Celsius,* and the day is *18 hours long*. It has 27 moons and also has faint rings around it. It takes 84 Earth years to orbit the sun, and it's the coldest planet in our entire Solar System.

Neptune: 4.5 billion km. from the sun with six rings and *13 moons.* Neptune is a gassy and icy planet with an average *temperature of -214 degrees Celsius.* A *day lasts 16 Earth hours,* and it takes165 years to orbit the sun.

Oumuamua

I'll conclude our look at the universe with a story gaining quite a bit of momentum through social media. Serious Astrophysicists have discovered an interstellar object careening through our solar system. The 'thing' has been named Oumuamua, and now scientists can see some fascinating observations with this unusual entity.

Oumuamua was first discovered in 2017, and it appears to be projecting an anomalous trajectory and acceleration. This has led experts to believe that the object cannot be confirmed as a natural phenomenon. This floating, rock-shaped object just may have been engineered by extra-terrestrial life forms. This should fascinate us, as it appears the years and years of waiting for confirmation on alien existence may be closer than we're even ready to accept or understand quite yet.

So, go somewhere quiet and hold your loved one's hand. Lie on the cool grass together on a clear, dark night and stare at the universe. Think of your parents and your siblings. Gaze at the unknown, and appreciate your place within it. It could simply be '*The True Meaning of Life.*'

"Then I heard another shot which hit him right in the head, over here, and his head practically opened up, and a lot of blood and many more things came out."

- Abraham Zapruder

A Cognitive Project

The J·F·K· Assassination

Now we'll move on to another conspiracy theory that goes way back. This event happened eight years before I was even born, and there are still two sides to the story. One is 'official,' and the other seems to make more sense. All I'll be doing in this chapter is offering my hypothesis of the event. Like 9-11, there are similarities.

We know that President John Fitzgerald Kennedy was assassinated in Dealey Plaza in Dallas, Texas, on November 22nd, 1963. We know for sure that the President was shot in the neck before the fatal shot to the head. Some of you may have seen the news footage as it was taking place, and others, like myself, have studied the material and broken down the day's events to understand, thanks in part to the infamous Zapruder film. This silent eight-millimetre moving picture is the most compelling evidence *against* the official report.

I have a good friend who has been there recently. He, too, is a firm believer that the fatal shot came from the Grassy Knoll. In the tranquillity of today's Dallas, he could envision that day and stood where the deadly shot happened. You can even go to Google Earth and see the distinguished 'X' that marks the spot of the most controversial, modern event before nine-eleven, 2001.

The J.F.K. Assassination

My friend told me that I would need to go there myself to get a proper understanding of how the tragic event took place, and I think he's right. I can do the research, watch the countless videos, and even listen to everyone's opinions until I'm blue in the face, but the truth is unless you've seen the site where it happened, in person, all you can do is share an opinion on the topic. A cognitive judgement that will hopefully someday be substantiated with some concrete proof. Whatever your opinion on the J.F.K. assassination, there is some sort of a cover-up. Whether it be about the suspected shooter, Lee Harvey Oswald or the various organizational levels said to have been involved. Someone still knows the absolute truth, and it will come out sooner or later.

To be fair, we should start this all off with the Warren Commission's official report, which they distributed, in completion, on September 24th, 1964. The information itself is 888 pages long, but these are the highlights. This is what the world was told after that faithful day in United States history, and this is the exact reason that conspiracy theorists have fought for better, definitive answers. They argue that the official evidence in the case just doesn't make sense. And it stems from the way the President's head snaps back and to the left at the time of the fatal shot. The Warren Commission states claim to irregularities in the report that seem to contradict this.

- *"The shots which killed President Kennedy and wounded Governor Connally were fired from the sixth-floor window at the southeast corner of the Texas School Book Depository."*

- *"President Kennedy was first struck by a bullet which entered at the back of his neck and exited through the lower front portion of his neck, causing a wound which would not necessarily have been lethal. The President was struck a second time by a bullet that entered the right-rear portion of his head, causing a massive and fatal wound."*

- *"Governor Connally was struck by a bullet which entered on the right side of his back and travelled downward through the right side of his chest, exiting below his right nipple. The bullet then passed through his right wrist and entered his left thigh where it caused a superficial wound."* The infamous 'Magic Bullet.'

- *"There is no credible evidence that the shots were fired from the Triple Underpass, ahead of the motorcade, or from any other location."*

- *"The weight of the evidence indicates that there were three shots fired."*

- *"The shots which killed President Kennedy and wounded Governor Connally were fired by Oswald."*

The J.F.K. Assassination

- "The Commission has found no evidence of conspiracy, subversion, or disloyalty to the U.S. Government by any Federal, State or Local official."

- "The (Warren) Commission could not make any definitive determination of Oswald's motives."

- The Warren Report/Wikipedia

Do you think this is the way it actually happened?

What we saw was quite clear indeed. The President's motorcade rounds the corner onto Elm St. at about 12:30 in the afternoon and waves to the crowds of adoring fans. As he approaches the infamous Grassy Knoll, a shot rings out. The first bullet that supposedly misses the motorcade altogether. Then another hits the President in the back of the neck. This has been coined by the conspiracy theorists as 'The Magic Bullet.' This same bullet travels through the President and enters the back of Governor Connally. The bullet then apparently exits the Governor's chest, shattering his right wrist and comes to rest, causing a superficial wound in his left thigh. This story in itself is difficult even to fathom.

Seconds later, the fatal, piercing shot was heard, and the wounded President had been struck in the head and killed. The report says the bullet entered the president from the back of his head and exited through the front.

Most conspiracy theorists believe the bullet entered from the front and exited the back. They claim the deadly round was fired from the Grassy Knoll. If it didn't happen this way, Oswald would have needed to reload fast. The limousine carrying the President and the rest of the motorcade then speeds off under the overpass (that other theorists believe a shot may have been fired from.) They then proceed to the Parkland Memorial Hospital.

Let's take a closer look at the suspected assassin, Lee Harvey Oswald. Did he seriously mastermind this intricate hit himself, or was he a minion in a grand crime?

Lee Harvey Oswald

He was born in New Orleans on October 18th, 1939. At the age of twelve, he was placed in juvenile detention for *truancy*. He was assessed as emotionally disturbed and attended twenty-two different schools growing up.

When he was seventeen years old, he joined the United States Marines. Oswald was court-martialed twice and jailed before being dismissed from the core. He defected to the *Soviet Union* in October of 1959.

Lee Harvey Oswald returned to the United States in 1963 with his wife and small child in tow. The young family decided to settle in the city of Dallas, Texas. It was then that Oswald might have been heavily involved in a strategic plan. A wicked plot to take out the President of the United States. He would have been a perfect killer.

He was found leaving the Book Depository after the shooting and supposedly left the rifle and some bullet casings on the sixth floor. Forty-Five minutes after the assassination, Oswald, at the age of twenty-four years, brutally shot and killed Dallas police officer J.D. Tippit on the street when he was questioned. He slipped into a movie theatre where he was later arrested for the murder of J.D. Tippit and transported to the Dallas precinct.

After pressure to find Kennedy's killer as soon as possible, Oswald was immediately charged with the murder of the President and held for questioning. Two days later, Lee Harvey Oswald was shot and killed on live television by Dallas nightclub owner Jack Ruby when being transferred. Obviously, to shut him up.

Now, if I knew nothing else about the events that took place that day, I would be convinced that Lee Harvey Oswald would fit the profile of an assassin perfectly. He was socially awkward, manipulated and most likely influenced easily. He would do anything to care for his family, and he was able to leverage his military training as a way to seal the deal. An easy choice for a group that didn't want to get blood on their hands. The truth is, however, that Oswald may have never even fired a shot.

A Cognitive Project

I would imagine that Lee Harvey Oswald was offered an enormous amount of money for the times, and all he had to do was shoot the President from the sixth floor of the Book Depository, escape without being captured, and collect his luxurious reward. We can sit and speculate on Oswald's motive, but he had no allegiance to Kennedy and knew he could do the job. My guess is that his conspirators didn't trust that *he could* do the job. This plan would have had at least one backup strategy, and if we look at the theories, there may have been a plot to ensure the job was done no matter what. This may or may not be an accurate depiction of the events. If I had to guess, I would speculate that Oswald was fooled into taking part, but the assassination had already taken place before he realized it, and as he said, he was used as a 'Patsy' or a scapegoat for the deadly task. Now we know what we've been told; let's look at what *most* are saying.

The Conspiracy Theories

Believe it or not, there are genuinely more than fourteen different 'accepted' theories of what happened that day. In all, there are many more proposed. Some of them were unbelievable, but I looked at all of them with an open mind. Between these fourteen theories and the official Warren Commission's report lies the truth of what transpired that day. Some speculate that multiple gunmen or snipers were used, and they were strategically placed around Dealey Plaza. The Warren Commission says that three shots were fired, but acoustic evidence suggests more bullets were fired. Other theorists suggest that a pedestrian holding an umbrella shot a poisonous dart into the President to stun him and slow the motorcade for the fatal gunshot. Still, others swear that Kennedy's limousine driver himself turned and shot the President point-blank. Even a claim that two bullets simultaneously hit the President. One from the front and one from behind. Still, others believe there could have been as many as twenty-six gunmen involved. Like I said, some of these theories are pretty absurd. The actuality is like a complicated puzzle, but one of these conspiracy theories has survived the test of time. As mentioned, this is the version that most people in the United States still believe to be closer to the actual truth. *The fatal shot came from the Grassy Knoll.*

The Grassy Knoll

As the President's car rounds the corner onto Elm Street, the intricate plan is in place after months of pre-planning, crossing every 'T' and dotting every 'I.' Like Oswald himself said, he was a 'Patsy.' He was told he would be one of the gunmen who took out the President. But the gunmen were already in place, and it was easy to frame Oswald. It's even possible that Oswald wasn't even responsible for killing police officer J.P. Tippit.

A Cognitive Project

As the motorcade drives through Dealey Plaza, a shot is heard from the rear or the Book Depository. It's said to miss, but another attempt is heard, this time from the Grassy Knoll. The President has been hit in the neck, which catches everyone's attention in the car. Including Governor Connelly, who shows no signs that he's been struck until a second later. An innocent man was said to be grazed in the face by another bullet coming from the rear. This as well would have missed. The man was standing under the triple overpass on Elm. And then, before the secret service can react, another shot rings out, striking the President in the head and killing him instantly. Most people still agree that this final, fatal shot came from the infamous Grassy Knoll. The unheard truth is that at least *fifty-one* witnesses who were interviewed, only minutes after the shooting, swore they heard the shots ring out from behind the wooden picket fence on the Grassy Knoll. No one ever testified in a court of law.

The Zapruder film clearly shows the President's head moving violently backwards and to the left. A terrorizing explosion of his head is evident and we can see the majority of the brain matter and blood escaping from the *front of his head*. This would indicate that the shot came from the limousine's front and not from behind as the Warren Commission's report would suggest. Doctors at Parkland Hospital all agreed that a great majority of the

President's rear portion of his head had been blown out. This would be evidence of a ferocious exit wound.

As a guy who wanted to figure this one out, I found a few things that debunk the *front theory's shot*. I don't necessarily believe these claims, but they do hold some weight and should be measured. These claims are what make finding out the truth a real challenge at times.

A doctor, who was sworn under testimony, was asked about Kennedy's movements after the slug's impact. He acknowledged that the President's back might have spasmed when the bullet entered the back of his head. This response would cause his head to snap back and to the left, which was consistent with the rear angle

Another professional, independent source admitted that the spray of blood we see in the Zapruder film is actually the exit wound which is always much larger than the entrance wound. This would be consistent with a shot from behind, but the damage was so devastating that even the doctors couldn't *initially* agree where the exit wound was. It was determined later during the autopsy.

Another medical expert said that Kennedy's head seems to move slightly forward, milliseconds before the shot's impact on the head. It suggested that the car had braked after the first shot, and Kennedy's head was simply reacting to the momentum of the slowing vehicle.

A Cognitive Project

But wait...this statement strengthens the conspiracy theorists. In 1979, new testimony started to surface that suggested the Warren Commission didn't do a perfect job with the initial investigation. These new findings drove a wedge between the one gunman theory and the evidence that seemed to support the fact-checkers.

Upon revisiting the J.F.K. investigation, the House Select Committee on Assassinations said that a conspiracy most likely caused the murder of the President. They also concluded that there were four shots fired. They would come from the Texas School Book Depository, the Dal-Tex building, and the Grassy Knoll.

Despite this testimony, the Warren Commission's report still stands as President Kennedy's assassination's authorized account. The trying case was reopened once again in 1998 by the J.F.K Assassination Review Board, who stated that prior investigations, more than likely, contained inconsistencies. They contended that (as previously thought) the photos taken of the brain, post-mortem, were probably not those of Kennedy's brain. There appeared to be a cover-up from day one.

They did discredit the 1979 account of the audio file captured by one of the police motorcycles. This is the audible evidence that claimed there were multiple shots fired. Regardless, their testimony on the findings of the

President's skull tells an undeniable truth. Doctors from both the Parkland Hospital and the Dallas Mortuary prove that the head had a 'massive cavity' at the rear of the President's skull without a shadow of a doubt.

This evidence alone supports the Zapruder film and shows a very obvious exit wound. In this case, the shot came from the front of the car and may put a dagger in the official report about the assassination. Perhaps, when the absolute truth is finally known, the history books might change, but there was so much more to this tragic series of events. All documents referring to that day have been legally ordered to be released in full and unredacted by *October 21, 2021*. But if this incident was a conspiracy, who did Lee Harvey Oswald conspire with?

The Warren Commission concluded that Oswald acted alone. Investigators supported this from the *Dallas Police Department*, the *FBI*, the *United States Secret Service, as well as* the *House Select Committee on Assassinations. (The same committee that changed its mind in 1979.)* There is, however, compelling evidence that implicates other organizations as being involved. These would include the *Central Intelligence Agency* (CIA), the *Dallas Mafia*, Vice President *Lyndon B. Johnso*n, Cuban Prime Minister *Fidel Castro*, FBI Director *J. Edgar Hoover*, and even the *KGB*. All of them had their plausible motives to take Kennedy out.

A Cognitive Project

Let's look at them individually and see their alleged involvement when it comes to this series of events.

The CIA

The director of the Central Intelligence Agency in 1963 was John McCone. He had been long suspected of withholding vital information about the assassination from the Warren Commission. As of 2013, the CIA has even admitted to this. McCone testified that Oswald acted alone, and there was no evidence of a conspiracy. The CIA was under scrutiny because of the President's decisions in Cuba during 'The War of Pigs.' Other motives would include Kennedy's firing of former CIA director Allen Dulles. Also, Kennedy's refusal to offer air support to the Bay of Pigs invasion. Kennedy had considered reducing the agency's budget by twenty percent, and they thought the President was weak when it came to communism. It was on top of the newscasts.

The Mafia

We know that Jack Ruby shot and killed Oswald in the basement of the Dallas police department. He was being transferred to another jail when Ruby jumped out of the crowd and put a bullet into Oswald's stomach. It was seen live by thousands of people on live TV, and at first reaction, most people were probably relieved that the President's killer got what was coming to him.

The J.F.K. Assassination

Jack Ruby was a Dallas nightclub owner, and his motives for shooting Oswald have been scrutinized over the years. Some believe that Ruby did it to boost his popularity and show America that a vile monster like Oswald shouldn't survive to see a jury. We know that Jack Ruby had ties to the mafia, and it would make sense to me that if they were involved in this conspiracy, someone needed to keep Oswald's mouth shut before he implicated any of the other participants of this scheme.

Conspiracy theorists believe the mafia was involved because of the hostility created when JFK's brother, Robert, began campaigning to stop the mafia's influence on the Teamsters, which Jimmy Hoffa led. Robert Kennedy started a relentless campaign on the attacking of organized crime. It's thought that Hoffa may have been involved in an original plan to take out Robert Kennedy, but we know what happened to JFK's brother when Sirhan Sirhan shot him in a similar eerie fashion.

Eye-witnesses on that day told reporters that Jack Ruby was seen behind the fence on the Grassy Knoll. He was identified as being there with Clay Shaw (aka Clay Bertrand.) Clay Shaw was subpoenaed to the courts in 1967 by the district attorney, Jim Garrison, who believed that Clay Shaw was the '*Clay Bertrand*' mentioned in the Warren Commission's Report. Jim Garrison implicated Bertrand in a detailed conspiracy involving many more participants. The cagey mafia supported the likes of Oswald, Clay, and Ruby, as well as other members who oddly died soon after, along with many of the witnesses who knew the plausible truth. Coincidence? It could be.

Lyndon B. Johnson

The Vice-President of the nation, at the time, wanted to be the President of the United States. Johnson was a staunch supporter of what their brave troops had already accomplished in Vietnam. Kennedy was very close to pulling the troops out of Asia, but Johnson retracted Kennedy's wishes and pushed further into Vietnam with increased troops once he was gone. History tells us that America never had a chance in Vietnam, but Johnson knew that war boosted the economy, and Kennedy didn't handle the *War of Pigs* suitably. Communism couldn't win, and Lyndon Johnson was said to have ordered the hit on Kennedy himself. It's now been discredited, but he would have had the power to react to the death and fallout, protect the others, and take over the country.

Fidel Castro

In 1961, JFK was unsuccessful in overthrowing Fidel Castro, the Cuban leader. At that time, the mafia controlled the casinos on the island, and they were forced to shut things down. It angered the American crime families who had financed millions of dollars to create a tourist destination that would rival Las Vegas. Theorists suggest that Fidel Castro himself had a definite desire to remove Kennedy from power, and ultimately this may have led to Jimmy Hoffa and the mafia conspiring.

The KGB

It's evident that Lee Harvey Oswald was involved in one way or another. He had tried to defect to the Soviet Union, but he was denied citizenship. When he lived in Russia for a short time, he was involved in meetings with the KGB. Some will even say that Oswald, who had a military background and was considered a sharpshooter, gained some advice from the KGB on ensuring a clean and effective shot. The CIA also said they intercepted a call from Oswald to Russia's KGB department in charge of 'sabotage and assassination' shortly before the murder of President John F. Kennedy. It seems very strange.

Three Shots in 8.3 Seconds with a Crappy Rifle?

The mysterious rife found on the sixth floor of the Book Depository after the shooting was never tested. It wasn't investigated or forensically verified. They located it beside four alleged shell casings. The window had an obscured view of Elm Street because of a tall and thick tree. In fact, the most precise shot for a single gunman from that location would have been when the motorcade was coming up Houston Street before the turn onto Elm.

A Cognitive Project

During some of the early investigations, several sharpshooters tried to replicate Oswald's alleged actions. None of them could reproduce the three shots in succession, accuracy, and time frame. Military experts have since simulated this feat, but we can't take the human element out of the equation. If Oswald were the shooter, he wouldn't have been calm, like a test shooter would have likely been. Although the commission says that the first shot missed, the likely- hood of the last two bullets hitting a moving target in the suspected time has been confirmed as 'nearly impossible.'

On top of this, doctors found a mysterious, unfired bullet on JFK's stretcher at the hospital. Theorists say it was planted, and I can't figure out the significance of this odd discovery. There may have been multiple outlooks ensuring the plan wouldn't fail, and the unusual seizure suffered by a pedestrian on the sidewalk, only minutes before the brutal shooting, would have commanded the attention and confused the Dallas police lining the street.

Here's what I think happened...

Most of my meek opinion is similar to the allegations presented by Jim Garrison back in 1967. This critical case was featured in Oliver Stone's 1991 movie, JFK. I will admit that I watched the film shortly after it was released, but I did not conclude my lengthy hypothesis and research from the movie much at all. Even I can understand that Hollywood glorifies their subjects, and everything in that film may not have been entirely accurate. These opinions are available online for anyone to study, but this makes the most sense to me.

I believe the plan had been in place for quite some time. Meetings were held, and a team of assassins was put into place. The claims of militant gunman used in the deed hold some water for me. These men would have triangulated their positions, a combat tactic used in ambushes for hundreds of years. In my opinion, I would agree that the men were planted at the Book Depository, the Dal-Tex building and the fence on the Grassy Knoll. It's possible that another gunman could have been positioned on the triple overpass. It would be the final chance for an execution if the other shots missed the President while the motorcade sped away. I would be guessing on the number of shooters, but in this case, I'd imagine that there were at least three or four.

As Kennedy's limousine turns onto Elm Street, he is in the middle of the sweet zone, surrounded by all suspects. The pedestrian who had the seizure was paid to fake the event. It distracted the police and allowed all shooters to secure their planned-out positions and ready their deadly weapons. At this point, they waited for the 'Go' signal, and their shots were strategically planned.

A Cognitive Project

The first shot came from behind. I imagine this bullet was shot from the Book Depository, but not from the sixth floor, and not by Lee Harvey Oswald. At this time, Oswald was in the Book Depository's cafeteria, enjoying a Coke and awaiting further instructions. The first bullet misses and could have possibly been the bullet that grazed the man standing near the triple overpass.

I think the second shot came from the Grassy Knoll and entered Kennedy's neck from the front. That would support the autopsy photos showing a small opening in the neck, and that bullet may not have exited the neck. At this point, in the Zapruder film, Governor Connolly hadn't been struck yet. He was holding his hat with the hand that the 'Magic Bullet' had supposedly struck. It would be the same bullet that hit Kennedy in the neck.

At this point, Kennedy stops waving and grabs his neck. His wife, Jacqueline, notices that something is wrong, as does Connelly and his wife seated ahead of them. The driver also hears the first shots and gently touches his brakes; as secret service agent Clint Hill runs to intercept the President's car and leap onto the trunk to shield Kennedy and his wife with his own body.

During this time, a third bullet rings out from the Dall-Tex building, striking the governor in the back and travelling through and exiting. It's believed that another, separate bullet also hit Connelly, explaining the multiple wounds on his body. It would have all taken place in a matter of seconds, and the shots would also create echoes that would fool people into thinking there may have been more or fewer shots fired at the scene than there were.

We then see the final shot come from the front of the motorcade and the Grassy Knoll. Far too many people reported the distinct sound of gunfire, with others seeing gunsmoke rising from behind the fence on the Knoll. This shot hits Kennedy directly in the frontal lobe, causing him to move back and to the left dramatically.

As Clint Hill finally arrives at the lead limousine, Jacqueline is already heading onto the trunk, retrieving her husband's brain matter while in shock. She is pushed back into the bloody seats, and the motorcade speeds off without another shot fired. The chaos that would ensue is unimaginable, but the gunmen quickly pack up their weapons and disperse the area in separate directions.

Oswald was still in the Book Depository and told by an employee that the President had just been shot. Oswald may have felt immediately shunned. Or maybe the plan went south, and they had to look after it before he was able to get involved. Oswald would calmly leave the Book Depository shortly before it was locked down, get on a bus, and then take a taxi to a muster point.

In this case, the meeting place was the movie theatre that Oswald entered. It could have been a place Oswald was told to meet after the job was done, and maybe he was planned to be murdered as a pawn to keep his mouth shut. But they would have been beaten there by the police. I believe Oswald didn't kill J.P. Tippit at all. It could have been another suspect who had the run-in with the policeman, but at that time, police had an all-points bulletin, looking for a man they hadn't seen yet. Any strange activities after the assassination would have triggered the authorities to jump to conclusions, and questioning the Book Depositories staff after the rifle and ammo were found on the sixth floor, made Oswald the prime suspect. The police were under tremendous pressure to find out who was responsible and appease the stunned nation. Some were shocked and saddened, while others sang from the rooftops after Kennedy was killed.

Two days after the shooting, Jack Ruby killed Oswald in cold blood. It would shut him up and keep his secrets deep inside his soul for eternity. I'm pretty confident that if Ruby hadn't succeeded, Oswald would have spilled his guts and fully implicated every participant in the evil plot. He was too meek and afraid to stay quiet for long.

If I had to take an educated guess, I would presume that Jack Ruby may have pulled the final trigger from the Grassy Knoll while standing beside Mister Clay Shaw.

The J.F.K. Assassination

After everything has been said and done, John (Jack) Kennedy's assassination on November 22nd. 1963 was a sad day in American history. It will be interesting to see if any new facts continue to trickle down over the coming years. The Kennedy family has surely been plagued with tragedy, and many of the members of that family have encountered untimely death. In fact, in the following years after the shooting in Dallas, not only did Robert Kennedy lose his life to an assassin's bullet but so did Martin Luther King Jr. in the same way. All of them had grand plans for peace and change. And each of them was killed by corrupt people who just didn't want to accept change. Afraid of the unknown and pressured by peers.

I'll finish this section with my humble opinion on an interesting video I watched about Ladybird Johnson. The wife of former President Lyndon Bains Johnson. Some aren't aware that Mr. and Mrs. Johnson were sitting in the limousine two back from the President, Jaqueline, Governor Connelly, and his wife on that day in 1963.

In Ladybird's recorded diary from that day, she says something fascinating. In her sweet southern charm, she reminisced about the shots she heard on Elm Street. She remembers a shot ringing out above her and to the right. It would have come from the Book Depository. And then she speaks of two more shots, on top of each other and almost consecutively. It verifies *at least* two shooters.

A Cognitive Project

The John F. Kennedy assassination will continue to be debated, even after more facts are revealed. It's a perfect example of how our history has fooled you into believing specific criteria that may not even be close to the truth. If Lee Harvey Oswald was indeed the 'Patsy' that he confessed before his death, he probably wasn't involved in the fatal sequence of events. If specific and primary investigations would have been handled a little bit differently, Lee Harvey Oswald could still be alive today. And he wouldn't have done time for the murder of John F. Kennedy. He would have done time for conspiring to kill the President of the United States, and the actual killer or killers would have been apprehended.

I didn't know the guy. I wasn't alive when he was, but I've read about him, and I understand what he stood for. I'm not even an American, but I personally look at J.F.K. as an honourable man who had ambition and empathy. He wanted to stop the futile war in Vietnam, and he was willing to speak up and challenge the system while others cowered and conspired. I would have been thrilled to have him as my President, but that's what always seems to happen. People who strive for change and peace are often eliminated by the weak, frightened lovers of war. It's a hunger that many humans possess, and it changes political views, leading to more chaos and detest within the mighty ranks of world government.

"History fades into fable; fact becomes clouded with doubt and controversy; the inscription molders from the tablet: the statue falls from the pedestal. Columns, arches, pyramids, what are they but heaps of sand; and their epitaphs but characters written in the dust?"

- Washington Irving

A Cognitive Project

The Pyramids and The Megalithic

Megalithic

"Planetary Archeology relating to or denoting prehistory monuments made of or containing large stones."

— Wikipedia

The ancient pyramids of Egypt have always fascinated me. From a very young age, I wondered how long ago they were built and *how* they were built more recently. This chapter will be about the pyramids in Northern Africa and the many grand pyramids worldwide. Some of them are still being unearthed today. The pyramids are one thing, but there are structures on our planet that scientists can't even say for sure, their age, or who built them, or how many of them were even constructed with yesterday's technologies. It continues to be a riddle, but we're able to ask so many crucial questions still.

Were these structures built by human beings? Did aliens make them? Perhaps they were created by humans with the assistance of aliens. Or maybe they were built by a species that once existed and has since gone extinct. Whatever your belief, we'll now take a look at some facts that exist, and again we will have to bring science into the equation, but many generations want to know.

Starting with the Egyptian pyramids, the facts about them, the Sphinx and other ancient monoliths are subject for debate. The archeological finds are becoming more prolific, adding to the mystery. It proves to us that our education is constantly changing. Recent discoveries at these sites tell scientists that some of these structures could pre-date what was scientists initially thought. The mighty Giza pyramids would be no exception.

The Pyramids were said to have been built by the ancient Egyptian civilization around four thousand years ago. That would have been about 2,000 BC. These structures contain astonishing architecture and even share some astronomical anomalies that would be highly coincidental if not planned. But these variances are precise and massive. What else do we know thus far?

The ancient pyramids of Giza, in particular, have mesmerized scientists and ordinary human beings for as long as we can remember. Were these structures built as religious shrines or burial catacombs? The site has many final resting places, but more importantly, we have debated throughout generations *how* exactly these great pyramids were planned and constructed in the first place.

Even the remarkable technologies we harness today couldn't simply construct something out of bedrock, so precisely. And there's much more for us to consider.

A Cognitive Project

The most recent and retriable explanation about Giza's great pyramids is interesting on its own, but then again, how accurate is the following information? Ten years ago, I'd be reporting entirely different statistics.

The largest pyramid is located in Giza, eleven miles outside of greater Cairo, in Egypt. But it wasn't the first pyramid in the area to be erected. In fact, the pharaoh Djoser built a step pyramid a century prior. *The official record says that the pyramid was built sometime between 2560 BC and 2540 BC.* That's around 4,500 years ago.

The great pyramid was built for the second pharaoh of the fourth dynasty, *Khufu*. The other smaller pyramids on the holy site were constructed as tombs for Khufu's wives. Ironically, having such an impressive memorial built for him, the only known and confirmed statue of the Pharoah Khufu stands only a measly three inches tall.

Originally standing at four-hundred and eighty-one feet tall, the great pyramid has shrunk about twenty-five feet of stone caused by four millennia of erosion. The structure now reaches four-hundred and fifty-five feet.

The expansive Nile is five miles from the pyramids. It seems a long way to transport more than 2.3 million stones to construct. Some of these stones would weigh an astounding 2.5 tons on average. The entire pyramid is said to weigh 6.5 million tons. That's a lot of chiselling.

The Pyramids and The Megalithic

These rocks were said to have been quarried from as far as five-hundred and twenty-five miles away. The polished white limestone casing stones were collected and moved from a smaller quarry closer to the site. Many of these casing stones were dislodged during a strong earthquake. The other rulers and kings gathered them in order to build newer shrines in and around the Cairo area.

It has often been speculated as to how these massive rocks were placed, sculpted and polished. Some experts claim they used a series of ramps for maneuvering the substantial stones. Others say spiral ramps with linear staircases slowly inched each rock into the air, where bronze levers were used to place each stone intricately. It would have taken many men, many hours and years.

The Romans stated that the pyramids were built by thousands of slaves, but Egyptologists are confident that skilled labourers built the mighty pyramids. Twenty to thirty-thousand work hands that included stonemasons, engineers, architects, surveyors and other skilled artisans. The theory is that a small crew worked on the site year-round, and a more extensive construction force was summoned when the Nile flooded the surrounding valley, enabling them to use boats to transfer the stones.

The interior of the great pyramid contains three large burial chambers. These were to keep Khufu's treasures

A Cognitive Project

into the afterlife. Human remains and great wealth was said to be stored in these chambers until around the ninth century when constant looting took place. Khufu's red-granite sarcophagus was untouched out of respect.

Giza's great pyramids are both the oldest and only remaining of the original natural seven wonders of the ancient world. Some which are still not verified as authentic, such as the Hanging Gardens of Babylon, the Colossus of Rhodes and the Statue of Zeus at Olympia.

It was Khufu's grandson who constructed the second largest pyramid and the construction of the Sphinx, which has significantly deteriorated. It was Menkaure who ordered the third and smallest pyramid on the site.

The debate about the construction

Archeologists and Egyptologists to this day are still not sure how the pyramids were built. Most speculate that a series of pulleys were used to raise the rocks into place, but there's much more that needs to be considered here for me. I can understand that these structures served as an act of civil service by skilled labourers. I believe they would have been paid handsomely for their efforts. But these would be my questions. Millions of tons of rock were shipped to the site. Probably one or two stones at a time. Again, these rocks were massive and heavy. *How were they cut from the bedrock? And how were they individually chiselled to fit each other like puzzle pieces? How were they raised into place? And how are they so precise to the coordinates of our planet and our space in general?* Maybe they were built by aliens…

This claim has been highly speculated over the years. Why? Because we can't understand the above questions. It's written that the great pyramid took roughly twenty years to construct. Some of our current and moderate technologies today allow us to build structures faster, but could they stand the test of time? Will the Statue of Liberty still stand more than four thousand years from now? I'm guessing that aliens may not have helped with these conceptions, but perhaps another, more intelligent species than our own, could have assisted. Maybe this particular species has been wiped out, and the transcripts have been misconstrued, like other historical facts.

I'm not going to revoke the claims that the Egyptian civilization erected these megaliths, but I do question the exact time frame, which could very well be later than we think. And I question how it was done. Indeed, a fantastic feat, and you can't help but wonder how many lives were lost during the construction phases. But if you look from above, you can plainly see that the entire area is surrounded by deep-rooted cemeteries, tombs, mortuary temples and ancient causeways with Mastabas and pits for boats to deliver the stones. But this is a hot desert…

Among the other archeological finds recently in the area, scientists have proven that a high-water line once submerged lower parts of the pyramid. It can be seen through erosion patterns and proposes that the entire area was once a vast waterway. The closest source would be the Nile River, five miles away. Much has taken place in the last four thousand *or so* years, and it's possible that Giza was once involved in a great flood of its own. Amazingly, these monuments have endured the times.

Controversy, controversy, controversy...

Like every subject in this book, there is loads of controversy when it comes to the pyramids. Here are a few that I found interesting, and they make you wonder.

Some claim that the original pyramids were much smaller when first erected and underwent a complete renovation and extension in the eighteenth and twenty-sixth Dynasty. Unlike the Sphinx, the pyramids don't show the same weathered erosion. It would support a rebuilding phase that has since been forgotten by time.

Many still disagree about whether the rocks, once cut free, were dragged, lifted or even rolled into place. Of course, boat transport would have made the most sense at the time, especially if water was present there. But most agree that the timeline of construction may be a bit off. Archeologists are finding evidence annually.

The anomaly of the placement

A little-known fact about the pyramids is that they actually sit three miles from their original Earth positions. That's how much our surface has shifted from the Earth's rotation in the last forty-five hundred years. The pyramids were built with recognition to two bright stars in the Big and Little Dippers to align the pyramids.

The tombs are aligned from north to south with a factual accuracy of up to 0.05 degrees. It is also common knowledge that the three pyramids perfectly line up to the three stars in the belt of Orion's constellation.

These historical crypts are impressive, but they're not the only human-made pyramids on the planet. To be honest, there are some we haven't even discovered yet.

Other pyramids on our planet

The famed Egyptian pyramids have garnered the most exposed attention throughout our history, but the planet Earth has other pyramid-shaped testaments, and they span across many different countries. These would have been assembled by various civilizations, which begs the question, where did this type of construction originate?

One example is *La Danta, El Mirador*, located in Guatemala amongst some of the most tropical jungles on the planet. At its peak, it had a population of more than

A Cognitive Project

eight thousand people. Archeologists claim that this pyramid was built by the Mayan civilization around the sixth century BC. That would make this overgrown structure more than twenty-six hundred years old. It was revealed in 1926 but received little attention.

Or we can go and see the *Pyramid of the Sun*, located in Teotihuacan, central Mexico. It is one of the largest pyramids in Mesoamerica, with a grand height of two-hundred and forty-six feet and an astounding seven-hundred and thirty-three feet across. The name came from the Aztecs, who visited the city centuries after it was abandoned. It was completed in two stages, with the first stage beginning about nineteen hundred years ago.

And then there is the *Bent Pyramid* in Dahshur, Egypt. It was the second pyramid built by the Pharaoh Sneferu and has a mysterious architectural flaw. The pyramid rises from the ground at fifty-five degrees and then suddenly changes to forty-three degrees to the peak. The theory is that with the sheer steepness of the original angle, the weight became overbearing and forced the builders to adopt a shallower angle. It stands three-hundred and thirty-two feet high and looks quite messy compared to the other great Egyptian pyramids.

Pharaoh Sneferu's first pyramid, *The Red Pyramid*, is a much more attractive piece of architecture. It's Slightly

The Pyramids and The Megalithic

bigger than his second attempt at three-hundred and forty-one feet high. It was the largest pyramid in Egypt until the construction of the Giza pyramids. Dating back an estimated six thousand years ago, this was the world's first successful attempt at constructing a true pyramid.

And others haven't even been discovered yet. Some of these fabled structures came into ruin early after their construction. The civilizations moved on or died out. Some are completely covered in thick grass and layers of mud caused by erosion and years of mismanagement.

They exist, though, and it appears they were all built by human civilizations, but how and why are still questions that need definitive answers. Some even claim that these structures appear on the moon and other planets like Mars, but we will have to wait for confirmation on these claims like everything else. The pyramids around the world remain one of humanity's greatest mysteries. A great debate on a long history.

Other Megalithic wonders around the world

There are literally thousands upon thousands of real Megaliths around the world. These have been found in over twenty countries, and astronomers even claim that they exist on other planets and moons in outer space. I think I would need some more proof of those sites, but here's some on the Earth that I find the most interesting.

A Cognitive Project

Stonehenge – 5,021 years ago.

The magical county side of England boasts one of the most eccentric sites on our planet. Stonehenge has long been contemplated as to its purpose. Most believe it to be a religious monument. But the question on everyone's mind is, how was it built? There's not a rock quarry around for one hundred and eighty miles. How were these rocks cut, transported and placed into the ground five thousand years ago? This site is one of our grandest mysteries on the planet. Go, if you have the chance to go.

Stonehenge is a prehistoric monument located in Wiltshire, England, and entails an outer ring of stones about thirteen feet high and seven feet wide. These massive stones each weigh more than twenty-five tons. It also has horizontal lintel stones adorning some tops.

It is one of the most famous landmarks in Britain and has become a cultural icon. The rocks were said to be quarried from Western Wales, nearly two hundred miles away. The man and animal power must have been epic.

The site has since been restored and confirmed as an ancient burial site. It was added to the UNESCO'S list of World Heritage Sites in 1986 and is visited by thousands of tourists and locals each year. All of them stare and wonder in awe. It's such a remote place for a megalithic structure to stand and *stand* the test of time for centuries.

Drombeg Circle – 2,821 to 3,121 years ago.

Although the Drombeg stone circle isn't the most impressive of the planet's megalithic structures, it gives us an honest look at how people lived before the alleged timeline of Jesus Christ. The circle, located in County Cork, Southern Ireland, is also called *The Druid's Altar*.

The circle of stones consists of seventeen stones closely spaced and span thirty-one feet in diameter. Four of these stones have since fallen or been destroyed. It boasts a long recumbent (*horizontal*) rock, and the others have been placed to slope toward the recumbent stone. It's been purposely oriented to face south-west toward the setting sun, but the alignment is not precise.

The site was excavated in 1957-1958 and restored after an inverted pot was found in the center of the circle containing an adolescent child's remains, wrapped with a thick cloth. Again, these stones' placement and alignment make us wonder how these massive rocks were cut (and from where). How were they moved? How were they placed into the ground, and what tools were used to create the circle? The Drombeg Circle is located one mile from the Atlantic Ocean. It's believed to have been built by the Druids between 1,100 and 800 BC. I sometimes wonder how much manual digging was done and how their everyday lives played out while there.

A Cognitive Project

Callanish Stones – 4,621 to 5,020 years ago.

They are thought to be even older than the infamous Stonehenge site. The Callanish Stones are another example of this ancient architecture that existed even before the suspected construction of the mighty Egyptian pyramids. This ring of glorious stones is located near the village of Callanish, on the west coast of Scotland.

Numerous other ritual sites lay near the stones of Callanish and include at least three other stone rings, several arcs, alignments and single stones. These all lay within a kilometre of the central circle and were used for various religious rituals for around 2000 years.

The ancient circle contains thirteen stones with a central monolith near the middle. It alone is 4.8 meters high, 1.5 meters wide, and 0.3 meters thick and has two long rows of stones running almost parallel. There is also a present-day, chambered tomb about 6.4 meters long running between the central and eastern monoliths. It has been nicknamed the *Stonehenge of the north* but never received the same fame and popularity over the years.

Machu Picchu – 571 years ago.

Machu Picchu was constructed in Peru by the Inca civilization in and around the year 1450 AD. It was said to be abandoned in the year 1572 during the time of the

Spanish Conquest. It sits on a 7,970-foot mountain ridge in a tropical climate by the twisting Urubamba River.

Archeologists believe it was constructed for the Inca emperor, Pachacuti, who lived from 1438 to 1472. It was assembled with polished, dry stone walls and intricate detail. By 1976, thirty percent of Machu Picchu had been restored. This restoration continues, and this monument has been recognized as a UNESCO world heritage site since 1983. It's also one of the *New Seven Wonders*.

Easter Island – 521 to 1,621 years ago.

One of my favourite places that I've *never* been to date. Easter Island was miraculous years ago, but we seem to be *uncovering* (pun intended) new mysteries annually. Located off Chile, the island is famous for more than one thousand colossal statues called *Moai*.

The sculptured rocks are said to have been built by the early Rapa Nui people, but experts disagree on the exact timeline of when the local Polynesian inhabitants arrived. A 2007 study found the timeline to be about eight-hundred and twenty-one years ago.

There's a tremendous amount of rich history in the relatively short time the island was inhabited. But what's genuinely exclusive is that these precise monuments are enormous. Some may relate Easter Island to a bunch of strange heads sticking out of the ground, but time and severe erosion have been tricking our weak minds.

These were tall, full-formed sculptures at one point, and they surrounded the perimeter of the island. Not only has Easter Island gained the prestigious designation as a UNESCO World Heritage Site, but archeologists and excavators are still digging and finding the statue's bodies deep below the grasses and sacred rocky Earth. Easter Island is a volcanic island consisting mainly of three dormant and extinct coalesced volcano domes.

Carnac Stones – 5,321 to 6,521 years ago.

The Carnac Stones lie around the French village of Carnac, in Brittany, France. They are the most extensive collection of megalithic standing stones in the entire world and were cut from the local rock in the area by the pre-Celtic people of Brittany during the Neolithic period.

There are an estimated three thousand stones on the site, but some have been removed in recent years to make way for roads. The management of the site over the years has been a controversial topic for several decades.

Gobekli Tepe – 12,000 years ago.

This human-made wonder was built at the beginning of the Neolithic period, and it predates humanity's oldest known civilizations. The site is finished with more than two hundred pillars about twenty feet high and weighing up to ten tons each. It remains quite a mystery how this megalithic ground was constructed and precisely what type of functions were performed there over time.

Gobekli Tepe is located in Southeastern Turkey and was built in two distinct phases. It is indeed the oldest megalithic site known to man, dating to around 9,500 BC, and is said to predate Stonehenge by seven thousand years. Archaeologists estimate that about five hundred people were used to erect the heavy pillars at the time.

Hatun Rumiyoc – 700 years ago.

Hatun Rumiyoc is a pedestrian street located in the city of Cusco, Peru. Just like that of Machu Picchu, the architecture is immaculate and contains stones shaped with unimaginable angles, all fitting together ideally like a jigsaw puzzle. The wall also holds the celebrated *stone of the twelve angles,* a rock with twelve distinct angles, and it fits perfectly with the surrounding chiselled stones.

The wall was once part of the grand palace in the area, built by the Inca Roca. The palace was partly dismantled after the Spanish invasion, but one hundred and ninety meters still stand today, and the intricacy is astounding.

The reason I find this subject so fascinating is that we still know little about our humanity. If we take Gobekli

A Cognitive Project

Tepe, as an example, it was built twelve thousand years ago. That's only twelve-thousand years ago in the big picture, and that's not really long at all. If we as a species have been around for, say, an estimated two-hundred-thousand years, there's a big gap here that we're missing. This gap suggests that humanity would have built these structures for much longer than scientists are aware.

Most of this history is lost. Buried under multiple layers of earth and perhaps never to be found and excavated. Some of the earlier monuments may have been destroyed by natural disasters or cast under our shadowy seas. We may never know of more prehistoric shrines, older and more enigmatic, but we are lucky to preserve our history. An authentic look back at how people long before us lived their lives and honoured their loved ones. These structures brought them happiness.

I have to finish with a short but funny story. During my research phase on the great Giza pyramids, I asked a friend what he thought about the subject. Like everyone else, he had his cherished opinions and offered insight into my inquiries. It all made sense when I asked him how the pyramids were built, though. He thought for a moment, nodded his head and said, "Well, one thing is for sure…the pyramids were built from the ground up." *Thanks, Nick.* Unless aliens constructed them, I believe everyone will agree with your theory. :)

"In the world of the very small, where particle and wave aspects of reality are equally significant, things do not behave in any way that we can understand from our experience of the everyday world...all pictures are false, and there is no physical analogy we can make to understand what goes on inside atoms. Atoms behave like atoms, nothing else."

- John Gribbin

A Cognitive Project

Quantum Physics

I'll be candid with you. I know less about this subject than any other in this book. Not only am I *not* a genius on this topic, like some others are, but I honestly knew nothing about Quantum Physics until I was in my early forties. When it caught my attention, it really caught my attention, and for the first time in my life, I didn't look at physics as math. *But really, it's all about complex math.*

With astronomers' assistance and the proof of what we already know, scientists have come to some mind-boggling theories regarding our very existence. They show solid evidence that the reality we perceive may not be accurate at all. I'll explain in this chapter some of these discoveries, and if you weren't aware of them before, you should be after this piece. It might be a bit challenging to comprehend, but if we open our minds and think outside the box, we'll see that there's still so much for us to learn. The what-ifs are constantly calling out to us, and science fiction is becoming science fact.

We'll begin with the meaning of Quantum Mechanics, and then we'll look at a couple of theories that teach us exactly how each and everything in our universe moves. This includes everything from a blade of grass to a black hole and everything in between. We'll refer to these atoms and neutrons as particles, and they are a *moving* presence in everything that we can imagine in our lives.

What is Quantum Mechanics (Physics)?

One of the most profound pieces of evidence when it comes to Quantum science is the Particle Theory. This discovery would question the very reality that we know.

The Particle Theory

The Particle Theory explains how all matter (liquid, solid and gas) is structured and reacts under certain conditions. This theory contains five critical statements that were proposed through scientific observations.

1. All matter is made up of microscopic particles.

2. There is space between particles.

3. All particles in a pure substance are the same.

4. The particles in all matter are constantly in motion.

5. Particles are attracted to each other.

Some references include a sixth statement that reads, particles move faster and get further apart when heated. Basically, every single thing we interact with daily is comprised of these tiny particles. These particles can exist in different places simultaneously and make us think that our reality has been a magic trick all along.

A Cognitive Project

The quantum theory on the movement of particles could change the way we look at our truth. The basic principle is that all these *particles move differently depending on whether they are being observed or not.*

Quantum physicists set up several tests, and one of most successful, in particular, was monumental in the understanding of how our brains perceive what we see. Here's a closer look at what these scientists observed. When I first read this article, I was floored. If this were true, it would change the whole impression of how our brains and bodies react to life's everyday stimuli. Even if psychics don't interest you, the hypothesis from this study may suggest that life, as we know it, could very well be a hologram. Everything that we see, and everything that holds us together, including each particle in our elusive brains, may only appear in a waveform.

The Double Slit Particle Theory

A British Polymath who lived from 1773 to 1829 named Thomas Young set up a relatively simple experiment. We can remember from our studies that an experiment contains an observation, a hypothesis, and a conclusion. If retriable, this meek conclusion becomes a fundamental theory, and this has become the most plausible theory on our very reality, as we know it today. Numerous scientists have tested this experiment over the years, and all of them have come up with the same observations supporting Thomas Young's theory.

I'll explain this theory, not as Thomas Young did, but from a different source, which was the easiest for me to understand. These scientists and physicists wanted to see how these particles react to direct persuasion. First, they set up a central point of light and in a non-prismed technique. They then placed simple particleboard that contained two distinct slits and placed this vertically. Behind that, the scientists set up a screen to populate and document their observations. It was their starting point.

They began by shining the light toward the two slits and recognized that the light caused an *interference pattern*. That means the light was travelling through the left and right slits, but certain waves of light interacted with one another and causing the light to refract to a different place on the screen. Scientists could clearly see a pattern of how the light waves transferred to the screen behind. There were distinct areas through the first slit and distinct regions through the second slit, but there were also light patterns covering the same width, top to bottom. Although this light theory has been scientific knowledge for more than two hundred years, it allowed them to see the particles' simple properties in motion. These same particles make up everything around us, including our bodies, brains, and all within the cosmos.

A Cognitive Project

To make things a bit easier to understand, you can imagine the same experiment using a paintball gun. Imagine if there was only one slit in the board, and you fired the paintballs at it. The screen on the back would show one distinctive pattern where the paint has passed through the slit in the board. It makes sense so far, right?

Now we can add a second slit and fire the paintball gun again. What we see now are two distinct paint lines on the back screen. Some are passing through the left slit and others through the right to create a probable pattern.

When scientists brought this experiment down to a molecular scale is when things didn't start making sense. Instead of using an object or particle with fundamental matter, they decided to fire atoms at the board. That should show the same conclusion that they observed with the paintballs. We know that the paintball and everything else in the entire universe contain molecules, neutrons, protons, electrons and atoms. In this case, we'll use atoms and call them microscopic particles.

If you set up your front board with only one slit and fired the atoms toward the slot, the pattern on the screen was as expected, with almost every one of the particles occurring where the slit opens to the screen. But then, if we added a second slit and then fired the atoms again, something extraordinary happened, confusing everyone.

This time something miraculous occurred. When the atoms were fired against both slits in the board, the screen pattern was similar to light. An interference pattern was achieved, showing that the atoms not only appeared where the slits were but all over the screen's width, top to bottom. It showed us that every particle in our universe moves in a wave pattern, and because these waves can contain the same scientific properties on one end of the wave as the other end, perhaps there is more to the perception of our reality. Our brains are in charge.

Going a step further, they decided to monitor and count the atoms as they flew through the board's slits. This would tell scientists exactly which slit the particle was travelling through. When they did this, though, the back screen pattern was not an interference pattern at all. In fact, the atoms arrived on the board as expected, showing a prominent presence where the two slits allowed them. But how did the atoms change properties?

So then, they could try and fool the atoms into thinking they were being monitored. They left the counter within the experiment's direct surroundings but unplugged it so it couldn't count the atoms and watch them. Incredibly, the pattern on the back screen was an interference pattern again. It suggested to scientists that everything we perceive may not actually be there if we don't observe it. If this is a fact, everything we've ever

A Cognitive Project

believed in to be true may not have ever existed outside of our minds. Essentially, every single electron will cause a wave or interference pattern. So, what we've learned from this, is when we observe matter, the wave function collapses, and our brains see the object as it is. This theory would state that when we turn our backs to something, it no longer exists as a solid and relatable object but more as an interference pattern similar to the static we see on our televisions with awful reception.

It's something difficult to believe, but physicists are only scratching the surface. Every discovery allows us to ask more questions and feel comfortable in a more thorough truth. But what could this really mean to us?

Properly speaking, the objects described in quantum physics are neither particles nor waves but rather a third category that shares similar properties to that of waves.

Historically, one of the most controversial aspects of quantum mechanics is that it's impossible to predict the certainty of an outcome of a single experiment in the quantum system. Each prediction contains probability distributions from many repeated experiments.

The discovery of these waves containing the same information throughout the wavelength suggests that an outcome on one end of the wave is determined by the other end. To break this down to laymen's terms. *If a ball is travelling through the air, the particle wave may have moved, faster than the speed of light, to another location where a different ball is soaring through the air.* Physicists call this phenomenon, *Entanglement*. Consequently, the theory of entangled states turned out to be one of Albert Einstein's brilliant mistakes. He didn't think this was likely, but now we know different.

Sir Isaac Newton thought light was made of very small parts or particles, and initially, particles and waves were not supposed to exist simultaneously. Perhaps the universe is entirely random, as Sir Isaac derived. What our brains tell us becomes a reality and is trusted most times. This specifically speaks to my point in earlier chapters. We know so little about our brains that we have found comfort in our present reality. But we may not be prepared to discover and adapt to a different philosophy.

Perhaps the Matrix wasn't as far-fetched as we first thought. If everything we perceive is moving in wave formation, our reality could simply be perceived by our brains. For myself, alternate dimensions, time travel, and teleportation may exist and be possible. And it may very well be a quantum physicist who will discover it first.

If we as a species can understand quantum physics or its mechanics clearer, we can then appreciate the real possibilities of time travel or even teleportation, perhaps.

A Cognitive Project

Finally, harnessing these elusive wave movements and connecting the dots to our perception would lead to tremendous advances and possibly cause an even bigger problem that many of us have thought about over time.

If time travel were possible, it would potentially change our time continuum, as we saw in the movie, Back to the Future. Changing something in the past would most certainly cause a ripple effect that would change future events' probabilities. This flies way over my head, but if science says it could be possible, it's just a matter of time before humanity is better educated.

But we understand what we understand, and not a thing more. Our brains project our reality, and it may be perceived differently depending on who is witnessing it. It may not even be relevant to you because things are the way they are, as they've been, and most likely always will. Again, knowledge is power. To claim dominance on this planet and have a chance to live longer than the dinosaurs, we need to learn to adapt to different possibilities. Please keep an open mind and remember that we are only students. We learn every day and change our perceptions and opinions. These advancements will continue long after we are gone, and we can be gracious that we were able to be part of this bizarre theory's pioneering. With enough integrity, we can celebrate our place in evolutionary history and never be forgotten.

"Progress is impossible without change, and those who cannot change their minds cannot change anything."
- George Bernard Shaw

A Cognitive Project

Our Miraculous Earth

Of all the chapters in this book, this is one subject we, as a species, know the most about. The funny thing is that even the brightest people on the planet still don't know a great deal. From our oceans to the icy continent of Antarctica, we still have much to learn about Earth.

It's pretty easy to take our home for granted. We are born here, and everything we see and learn becomes 'normal' to us. The sky is blue, the mountains are high, nature is unpredictable, and the sun keeps us all alive. If we believe in miracles, the real miracle would be our proximity to our star, the sun, as aforementioned.

Our planet is so beautiful in many different ways. This beauty is a direct result of our atmosphere and the lifesaving rains that fall worldwide each day. But we haven't always had a landscape like this. As a matter of fact, the Earth has been through absolute hell, and it's been uniquely altered over the past *4.5 billion years.*

We'll now take a look at the Earth in a way you've never seen before. From its long history to humankind's evolution, we still have so much to learn, and it would seem, like most things nowadays, there will be debates and diverse opinions. But first, the most trending topic.

The Earth isn't flat...and it's not round either.

It's difficult for me to find any *concrete* evidence on the 'Flat Earth' movement. Anything is possible simply because we are still learning. If the last chapter told us anything, we might very well be observing everything in our existence differently than it manifests to us.

So, if the Earth isn't flat, it must be round, right? Well, actually, the Earth isn't perfectly round either. The planet has an oblate shape and expands around the equator as it wobbles and rotates on its axis. In actuality, if the Earth could stop and come to a standstill, it would look more similar to the shape of an Australian football.

Another scientific law comes into effect here too. Centrifugal Force will make all the planets we observe appear round because they are spinning so fast on their axis. It's so fast that we can't even see it with the naked eye. Even a cube or a wooden stick will appear round to the naked eye if they are spinning at very high velocities.

The Earth's diameter is 12,714 km, from pole to pole, and 12,756 km's around the equator. The melting glaciers are essentially causing the planet's waistline to bulge even more. And as global warming affects our ice shelves at an alarming rate, the globe stretches and theoretically becomes progressively unstable. The moon is gradually slowing down the Earth's rotation as well.

A Cognitive Project

A Brief, Four Billion Years of History

The Earth formed more than four and a half-billion years ago. Depending on your beliefs, this rock we call home came to be in several different ways. If you believe the *Big Bang Theory,* that could explain our infancy. Or maybe you believe that God created us. The Heaven's and the Earth, as stated in the bible. Or perhaps you feel that we came to be from a complex chemical reaction and collision in space that allowed all of the planets in our solar system to remain within the Sun's orbit. Even the moon itself could have collided with the Earth at some point, suspending itself close to our gravitational pull. The moon may have once been a part of the Earth. We still don't know for sure yet. Science continues to evolve.

Some will even claim that our moon is an artificial satellite, housing a secret base for extra-terrestrial life, but that's another project we can discuss in the future. The funny thing is that what I am researching today is entirely different information than I would receive if I examined the same subject five years ago. And five years from now, there will be brand new advancements and discoveries made. But this is what we think we know. As a matter of fact, the following is the most updated theory on our great planet's formation and lengthy history. The timeframe is in the millions of years, so this shows just how subtle the planet's changes can and have been.

Almost 5 billion years ago, the Earth didn't exist. We had the formation and birth of our star, the sun, and it was surrounded by space dust and small rocks. Over time, gravity pulls this debris into larger rocks, and after millions of years, the rocks smash together in a cosmic game of dodgeball, forming the planet Earth. But this is far from the planet that we are familiar with today.

At this time, the Earth was only one of more than 100 planets orbiting our sun. Most, of course, didn't survive the bombardment of multiple shifting collisions and were removed from the sun's orbit to float free in space. The Earth itself was a molten mass that resembled more of Hell than home, with a temperature of over 2000 degrees Fahrenheit. There was no air, only carbon dioxide, nitrogen and water vapour. Essentially, our planet was a boiling ball of liquid rock containing an endless ocean of lava. No life was able to exist yet.

A day on Earth is only six hours long at this point, and there is another young planet heading straight for Earth. Its name is *Theia*, and it's about the size of Mars. It speeds toward the planet at ten miles per second, or twice as fast as a bullet. This coincidental collision was necessary to shape our globe to that of today's vision.

Upon Theia's impact with the early Earth, both young planets turn to liquid. The energy created by the collision causes trillions of tons of debris to blast out into space. In only 1000 years, gravity makes this dust debris form into a ring that orbits the Earth. It would be similar to what we see around Saturn or Uranus now, for instance.

Over time, these rings slowly formed into our moon, which at that time is a mere 14,000 miles away. A far cry from the quarter of a million miles away nowadays. Earth is spinning so fast because of the new formation of the moon. Over the next millions of years, the moon slowly moves away from the Earth, and the planet cools.

Fast forward to 3.9 billion years ago, and meteorites begin bombarding the Earth with relentless force and repetition. These meteorites contain the debris left over from the vague assembly of our Solar System. But most importantly, when these meteors strike the Earth, they release tiny crystals about the size of salt grains. Each crystal contains minute traces of freshwater, which would become the essential piece of our living existence.

Over the next twenty million years, the meteorites continue hitting the planet with molten rock that contains some of the essential building blocks of life. But life is still unable to exist. There would need to be more time. The minute traces of water, over time, has created pools of water on the planet to grow. It allows the angry Earth to cool enough to form a robust and solid inner crust.

700 million years after its birth, the Earth is now covered in water. Meteorites still enter our gravitational pull, but they are less frequent now, and it would appear that the planet is beginning to settle and calm itself.

Tiny islands of land start appearing as if they were magic. These are formed by volcano's deep below the water surface. The magma creates volcanic rock that rises through the ocean and cools, comprising tiny land islands. These land formations are popping up around the globe and settling. But they are not yet stable.

The islands of land move and shift, colliding with one another and eventually, they form the first continents. Life, though, is still not possible. The atmosphere is toxic, and the surface temperature is still scorching hot.

But around 3.8 billion years ago, the meteorites came again, this time with more intensity, and the meteors would splash down in the enormous ocean that covered the surface. These meteorites contained the minute traces of water, but they had something else that, when mixed with freshwater, releasing some life-giving properties. These meteors would contain carbon, water minerals and primitive proteins with amino acids from outer space.

The waters eventually become a chemical soup, and over more time, the ocean fills itself with life. Single-celled, microscopic bacteria now control the vast waters.

A Cognitive Project

In the following hundreds of millions of years, not much with a lot of significance took place on the planet. It continued to be a hostile environment, but something miraculous was happening in the shallow ocean. The cold waters now contained many colonies of living bacteria called, *Stromatolites*. These bacteria are turned into food by photosynthesis, converting glucose, or simple sugars, into a remarkable by-product called *Oxygen*. It would become the framework for life as we know it today. Most importantly, it's the only reason we can breathe today. Something else we take for granted.

Over the next 2 billion years, multitudes of oxygen levels continue to rise and release changes into the atmosphere. The days are now sixteen hours long, but the surface temperature is still exceeding livable conditions.

1.5 billion years ago, the Earth's crust generated massive plates which begin to shift. In the next 400 million years, the plates have shifted the existing land into one vast continent that we've named *Rodinia*. The days are now eighteen hours long, and the planet's surface temperature has cooled to around eighty-five degrees Fahrenheit. The Earth is now oxygen-enriched, but the planet still had no complex life signs after more than three billion years. But once the building blocks of life were in place, it wouldn't take much longer for evolution to finally begin. It is like planting a tiny seed.

Fast forward again to 750 million years ago. Heat is escaping from the central core of the planet. It begins weakening and stretching the crust. The plates start moving again, in a destructive matter, and the supercontinent is spitting into two distinctive pieces of land. More massive volcanos erupt from the movement of the Earth's crust, and large amounts of carbon dioxide are released into the atmosphere. The carbon dioxide mixes with water and falls back as acid rain.

The shifting of the land has created large rocks that begin absorbing the acid rain. After a time, there isn't enough CO_2 in the atmosphere to trap the sun's heat, and the planet quickly starts to cool on the outside. Now, the timeframe would be about 150 million years later.

In only a few thousand years, the planet has been transformed into a ball of snow and ice. The Earth deflects the sun's light back into space, and the ice grows thicker and more rapidly. The temperature now dips to around -60 degrees Fahrenheit. The ice becomes an extraordinary 10,000 feet thick. The sheet covers the globe, and the sunlight can't penetrate. This first Ice Age lasts for about 15 million unforgiving, frozen years.

Eventually, even though the planet's surface is frozen, the core is still hotter than the sun. So more relenting volcanos break through the ice and spew tons more CO_2

into the atmosphere. The volcanos make a significant impact on the ice, and soon there are millions of tons of carbon dioxide, and with nothing to absorb it, the CO2 contaminates and fills the atmosphere. Soon though, the temperatures start to rise, and the ice begins to dissolve. Oxygen levels skyrocket again, and a chemical called hydrogen peroxide is produced. The hydrogen peroxide released enormous amounts of oxygen as well.

Around 540 to 600 million years ago, the days were around twenty-two hours long, and the temperature was similar to a nice summer day on the planet today. The ice age has finally ended, and in the oceans, the single-celled, primitive bacteria have not only survived the millions of frigid years, but they have highly evolved.

The seafloor is littered with green, lush plant life, and there's something else too. They resemble an armoured slug, and they scurry along the sand and rock under the water. They are called *Wiwaxia,* and amazingly, these are multi-celled organisms. For a brief period in our time continuum, Wiwaxia was the first animal Earth had seen.

And then, one of the Earth's most dynamic periods took place. We have called it the *Cambrian Explosion.* During this time, these creatures continue to evolve into larger and stronger aquatic animals. Eventually, they grow into a species that has a boney skeleton. They are called *Trilobites*, and these elementary animals would someday evolve and become the distant relatives of today's insects, lobsters, and even scorpions. Life in the oceans is blossoming, and oxygen levels continue to rise. This period in Earth's timeline shows to have introduced tens of thousands of sea life types to the planet.

Now, only 460 million years ago, the Earth's plates are moving again. This creates a new continent called *Gondwana*. This new landmass has nothing growing on it. There are small patches of moss on the mountain tops, but all other life still exists in the seas. The Earth is blasted by radiation from the sun. Nothing is protecting the planet from the deadly gamma rays entering the atmosphere and punishing the barren landscape.

Over the next 120 million years, the ozone layer forms, shielding the deadly rays from the sun. It allows more moss to grow on the hillsides, and it produces even more oxygen, allowing levels to skyrocket.

375 million years ago, we can start wrapping our heads around the timeframe of the planet. Creatures in the water have continued to evolve, and a fish called *Tiktaalik* rules the ocean with unusual intelligence. This fish has legs instead of fins and eventually moves out of the water onto dry land. They breathe oxygen, and over the next 15 million years, many more species evolve.

A Cognitive Project

And then, 360 million years ago, *Tetrapods* were introduced to the planet. They were the first four-legged vertebrates to exist. Now the trees and ferns are more than 100 feet tall. Their seeds blow in the winds and settle miles away, maintaining their own water supply. These seeds were able to live for years, and soon the oxygen levels on the planet are quite similar to today.

As more time passes, some new species arrive. Wings have replaced their legs, and they fly above the pleasant but still fluctuating Earth. These are the very first Dragonflies, and they're the same size as today's Eagles. Millipedes grow to be six feet long, spiders and other Arthropods are monsters, and scorpions are the size of wolves. The oxygen levels are much higher than they are today, and the species continue to multiply, introducing vicious predators and plant-eating prey alike. And a lizard-like creature called the *Hylonomus* is the first animal to lay eggs on land. These are the first reptiles.

Unfortunately, with life comes death, and now, 300 million years ago, the Earth is getting angry again. Many more volcanos erupt, and magma seeps through cracks in the Earth's surface. The massive, untouched foliage eventually weeps and dies, causing less oxygen and more CO_2 once again. These multiple layers of deadfall hold every piece of coal that we as human beings have used in our everyday lives since the late 1880s. Imagine that.

Now, 250 million years ago, the planet still rumbles, but life on the land is still evolving. The reptiles have become enormous and roam the land, feasting on the lush grasslands and becoming the world's first dominant herbivores. And there are even larger predators. Giant, lizard-like beasts with sharp teeth and razorblade claws. They are brutal killing machines and introduce the tragic and wonderous 'Circle of Life' as we know it today.

Inevitably, the imposing volcanic eruptions become more prominent, and lava spews high into the air and flows over large sections of the land, killing every living thing in its path. The entire landscape has erupted, and it will challenge the young species, both on land and in the waters. Even where life began has been compromised. It becomes well known as *The Permian Extinction*, showing us how easily a species can be snuffed out and just how precious our existence truthfully is.

On the distant side of the Gondwana continent, it appears to be snowing. It's lethal volcanic ash that has travelled 10,000 miles through the air. As it falls to the ground, it burns and suffocates the animals, killing them worldwide. Suddenly, life on the planet is in great jeopardy. For 50 million years, the Earth erupts, and it even affects the precious life in the oceans. These fierce explosions are coined *The Siberian Eruptions*, and Sulfur Dioxide fills the air, clouding the atmosphere.

A Cognitive Project

When it rains, the gas turns into Sulfuric Acid, and the water kills everything it lands on. Some animals have burrowed underground to survive, but many species have already completely disappeared. Now the Carbon Dioxide levels increase again, killing all plant life and reducing oxygen levels. The temperature gets hotter, and all of the water starts to evaporate around the globe.

The oceans turn pink and stripped of oxygen. Many species in the sea disappear. Methane gas escapes from the water and releases into the atmosphere. The air temperature now averages more than 105-degrees Fahrenheit. Ninety-five percent of the land species have been wiped out, and few land animals still live. The planet had now reverted to when it all began, it seems.

Now, only pink algae live in the ocean. It's the only thing that can survive. The eruptions last 500,000 years, and much of the Earth is now covered in lava. In some places, there is molten rock more than four miles deep.

During the Siberian Eruptions, the plates below the surface continue to shift catastrophically. Some massive mountain peaks are born as the land crashes into each other. 200 million years ago, the continents came together once again. This new supercontinent is called *Pangea*, and it reaches from pole to pole. The planet is healing, temperatures regulate, and life commences.

Now, a brand-new species has evolved. The reptiles that survived the Permian Extinction have transformed into Dinosaurs. At this point is when most humans can grasp our Earth's timeline. We're all well aware of what these beasts were able to accomplish on our planet.

The dinosaurs rule the Earth, but the plates are on the move again. 190 million years ago, Pangea broke apart. A vast chasm creates a new ocean called Panthalassa, which will become the Middle Eastern deserts one day.

Strong currents push nutrients up from the seafloor and into the warm upper waters. It attracts fish by the millions. But as always, death becomes a part of life, and in the next 10 million years, dead fish and plankton litter the ocean floor. They are buried by layers of rock and heated, transforming onto oil. Every gallon of gas, every piece of plastic, even the carpet we walk on, paint, and the soap we wash with all originated in this way.

180 million years ago, the North American plate was moving away from the European and Asia plates. The lands are shifting away from each other, one inch a year.

After another 35 million years, New continents form. The United States breaks away from Africa, and the giant chasm fills with water and becomes the Atlantic Ocean. The world is looking quite recognizable to what we see today, but sadly, the planet's chaos is far from over.

A Cognitive Project

In the middle of this new ocean lies an enormous volcano that breaks through the sea's surface and erupts with great force. The continental plates are on the move once more, and this time the seafloor tears in two and push up into a ridge of mountains and new volcanos. Some are higher than the Himalayas. A new ocean floor has formed, and the water temperature is hot and active. But life in the waters seems to flourish independently.

The Cretaceous residents of the planet have adapted and evolved into unique species. Some land animals have grown fins and gills, making their way from the land into the vast Atlantic Ocean. The Pliosaur is one of these creatures, and they develop jaws that are eight times more powerful than a great white shark. It's longer than a bus and contains razor-sharp teeth that are twelve inches long. With the Pliosaur ruling the waters and the Tyrannosaurus Rex reining the lands, only the strong would survive. The dinosaurs seem invincible.

After dominating the Earth for 165 million years, the dinosaurs have survived volcanos, earthquakes, and the shifting of the continents. But 65 million years ago, we're all quite aware of what happened to this species. They wouldn't have seen it coming, and it was extreme.

Nothing on Earth could have defeated the dinosaurs, but outer space had different plans. An Asteroid, larger than Mount Everest, and at least six miles across, screams into Earth's atmosphere at more than 40,000 miles per hour and changes the world forever. In a split second, the Gulf of Mexico incinerates from the impact. The rock hits the Earth with the same energy as millions of nuclear weapons. Thousands and thousands of tons of rock are ejected far out into the atmosphere, and the blast wave moves out in all directions, taking out everything in its path. Now debris circles the shattered Earth.

The debris rains down, hundreds of miles away from the impact zone, and pounds the planet with molten, fiery rock. There are numerous earthquakes and tsunamis as the blast cloud evaporates everything and moves around the globe. Molten rock spreads out, covering the Earth, and just like that, it has been transformed, once again, into a wasteland. Very few animals will even survive.

The planet reaches an insurmountable 500-degree Fahrenheit, and months after impact, black ash blocks out the sun's rays. Lush vegetation withers and dies or combusts spontaneously. Most of the surviving animals will starve to death. 65 million years ago, the dinosaurs were gone, and the Earth will need to heal once more.

A new species of small mammals have survived by hiding underground and adapting to the scorching heat. After 165 million years, the mammal is now the king.

A Cognitive Project

Only 47 million years ago, the Earth was peaceful. It had calmed again, and the plates continued to shift. The mammals had evolved. Their eyes and brains are larger, and they had adapted to their lush habitats. A brand-new species called Darwinius masillae, also known as Ida, resembles that of today's primates. This ancient animal species would become the first and early ancestor to the monkey, the ape, and eventually the human being.

The atmosphere is similar to today. The temperature has moderated to a comfortable 75 degrees Fahrenheit, and the days are just under twenty-four hours long.

But the seismic activity has increased again, and the planet will undergo another drastic makeover. India moves north toward Asia, and the tectonic plates crash together with extreme force, causing an epic buckling. The ocean floor contorts upward in a 1,500 mile-long line and creates mountain ranges 27,000 feet high. These are the Himalayas where we would find Mount Everest, and it stands as tall as modern airliners fly.

The mountains feed the Asian rivers as the snow melts from their altitude. Now, 20 million years ago, the planet is silent again. It now resembles how we see our continents today, but human beings are still missing.

At this point in our timeline is where some people are debating our arrival on the planet. There could be holes.

Four million years ago, new mountain ranges were formed by shifting plates and deadly earthquakes. The African coast opens up, and some ape-like creatures are forced from their habitats as their lush rainforests become savannahs. The temperature becomes agonizing.

Now, just 1.5 million years ago, the apes adapt and evolve. They stand upright instead of dragging their knuckles, and they learn to use tools. These are the *Homo Erectus*, and they will evolve into a dominant species.

70,000 years ago, the sea levels fell. It's thought that only two hundred of the Homo Erectus crossed the shallow Red Sea from Africa to the Americas. They would evolve into the *Homo Sabian*. The human being.

40,000 years ago, Europe was freezing, and massive sheets of ice start moving to the south. The Earth's temperature dives again, and the planet enters another ice age. Sea levels continue to fall, and in 20,000 years, the ice over North America is *one and a half miles* thick.

14,000 years ago, the ice started to retreat. The ice age had lasted a phenomenal 26 thousand years. Scientists believe we are slowly entering another ice age today. When we are immersed, our survival will be challenged.

The ice age created vast diversions in the ground. Water fills them, and they become the *Great Lakes*.

By six thousand years ago, all of the ice has retreated back to the poles. The human being multiplied, and now the planet is covered by nearly eight million of us. We remain in a constant struggle from our history. The Earth will freeze again, and it will be covered by fire again. Our time here is limited, but new species will surely survive after we are long gone. The next chapter in Earth's timeline is still to be written, as the planet still has around 4.5 billion years left before the sun expires.

Dissecting the timeline of human beings

For this study's purpose, I will join in on the many questions the human species' timeline, or perhaps a human-like species that may have walked our planet. If we look at the previous pages, we see that the Homo Sabian arrived around 70,000 years ago. However, there is consistent evidence that the human being has been around much longer than this. If I would have written this book five years ago, I'd be telling you that humans may have been around as many as one-hundred-thousand years ago. But today, scientists believe that we may stem back as far as two-hundred-thousand years. I think these dates will continue to move backwards over time.

If we consider only one-hundred-thousand years as a starting point, that timeframe could have spawned many other species that have since vanished with no evidence.

Every day, we are discovering new evidence that humans may have been quite different at some point. In fact, giant skeletons have been found with enormous heads. They would have stood between eight and twelve feet tall. These skeletons were found, yet the unusual beings don't seem to make the local news, and they certainly don't inspire the textbooks to change curriculum facts.

I want to quickly take a look at the last two-hundred to three-hundred-thousand years ago. Consider this time period and compare it to all the time you can remember and all the time you can recall from hearing of your ancestry. You may be able to find a lineage two or three hundred years back. Other families may have records that go as far back as five or six hundred years or more.

If we take a baseline of five hundred years back, that would be around the year 1521. Then we can understand the timeline of the bible that says Jesus was born 2021 years ago. Before that, we have read about history and many wars that shaped our religions and beliefs. We know of people who were around thousands of years before Christ, but even if we round this to 5000 years ago, we have to understand that humans, as we know it, were here on this planet more than two to three-hundred-thousand years before that. We haven't even made a dent in the timeframe. So, is it possible that we don't have a complete understanding of everything that once existed?

Maybe there was a species lost to the Earth that we haven't discovered yet. Like the giant species, or perhaps another that shared knowledge from outer space to build the pyramids and other megalithic structures. Hobbit species are said to have existed, and to be honest, the thought of a unicorn being something real was a definite possibility, in my opinion. I genuinely believe that when it comes to our brains, our reality, and our afterlife, we are still being educating and grasping. Researching and trying to establish the truth we have all been waiting for.

Earth's Natural Phenomenon

Living on this majestic planet does not shield us from the ultimate powers of Mother Nature. Our atmosphere is our lifeline, but it can produce a concoction that has wiped out entire species in the past, and it will continue to release its natural anger in the present and the future.

Volcanos

Fiery volcanos are located on every one of our seven continents. Some of them are dormant now, and others continue spewing lava creating molten rock, which adds daily to the Earth's landmass. A large volcano is active in Iceland right now, and one on the main island of Hawaii is also heavily erupting in a fuming fashion. These pits of hell are monitored, but their fiery contents can unleash a number of issues for the general area.

We know what happened here in North America when Mount St. Helens erupted in Washington state in 1980. The ash travelled for thousands of miles around. People died, and the mountain was reshaped in the blast.

There are much bigger and bolder volcanos that could explode at any time. Scientists have ground-breaking technologies in place now to predict these inner tremors at the earliest convenience. Still, nothing can stop the enormous destruction when the Earth opens up to release its molten core. If we look at our history, all is clear.

We saw earlier that volcanos had designed our planet, and they seemed to happen quite frequently. But we were looking at a timeline of more than four billion years, so they would have seemed to come in succession. That is how the continents have changed, and this is how the continents will change again in time. These volcanos help release pressures from inside the planet, and years after their destruction and harm to our environment, they allow the Earth to heal, rebuild itself and introduce some new life. The nasty volcano may be intimidating, but it truly is the reason we are here in the first place.

And of course, we can't forget Pompei. The sizeable Italian town stood beside the daunting Mount Vesuvius. In 79 AD, it erupted, sending ash and molten rock into the tiny community, killing everyone that stayed to face it. Women have been immortalized in stone, still holding their newborn child, and men have been sealed in time, lying in the fetal position and waiting for the end.

Earthquakes

Truthfully, there are hundreds of earthquakes around the world each day. Most are weak and unnoticeable, but others can be fierce, and we've seen throughout our history that earthquakes, along with volcanos, have shaped our planet. And when the ground shakes, it breaks. The plates collide, and the stress shakes the core of the planet. It would enable toxic lava to flow freely.

If you caught my last novel, Cascadia, I described one of the major threats on our planet. The Cascadia Faultline ruptures will cause death and destruction on the Pacific Northwest of North America. The next earthquake is estimated and predicted to be over 9.0 on the Richter scale. It will cause a tsunami that will reach Japan, Hawaii and Alaska in some dramatic fashion.

Even scarier is the too well-known San Andreas Fault located just south of the Cascadia line. When this rupture occurs, the death toll will be even higher, and the infrastructure damage will take many years to heal. Both the San Andreas and the Cascadia earthquakes will cause a ripple effect around the world that will make 9-11 seem sadly insignificant. And these ruptures are long overdue.

Of course, there are many other threats around the world when it comes to our Earth-shaking. There is no avoiding the fury of the planet, and there's even worse.

Hurricanes, Typhoons and Cyclones

Great forces can be created in our enormous oceans. These funnels of winds can reach speeds of more than two hundred kilometres per hour. In Asian countries, these phenomenal winds are called Cyclones. In the South Pacific, they're called Typhoons, and in North America, Hurricanes can be devastating, especially with little warning. These natural forces of nature are predicted and caused by wind patterns. They can be lethal out at sea *and* on the land that stands in its path.

These storms are categorized, and there isn't anything that we can do to stop them. Thankfully, we have gained the ability to prepare and mitigate the damage and, most importantly, the devastating loss of life. The power of the wind on our planet can be damaging over the land too.

Tornados

Tornados boast some of the fastest, wicked and most destructive winds on the planet. These land funnels are rated on the Fujita Scale, from an innocent F-1 to an incredible F-5 in intensity. In only minutes, these storms can wipe our entire localities and leave a trail of ruin.

A Cognitive Project

Fires and Floods

Perhaps the most common and destructive forces on the Earth are flash flooding and devastating fires. I think of the recent fires that torched Australia and the non-stop effort in California recently. I can remember the Amazon rainforest fires, and it saddened me to see such a majestic place burn beyond recognition. And then I saw a post, six months later, showing a tiny green sprout poking from the scorched Australian ground. It gave me hope and showed me that life would continue to flourish. But some live dangerously close to massive rivers and vast seas. The Earth doesn't care about your location. Water is one of the most powerful forces we encounter and has crippled thousands and thousands of populated places worldwide. Again, we do have some warnings with the water, but fire can certainly consume in mere seconds.

Over Population

The Earth is approaching a population of five billion humans. Our intellect and knowledge just so happen to be a major detriment to us. Money, greed, bloodthirst, selfishness, religion and misinformation plague us. The more people, the more troubling opinions and beliefs.

Luckily, most of the planet is governed by some sort of law, but the more people feel distressed, the more likely they will revolt against each other in the end.

Scientists have estimated that the Earth should be able to sustain as many as ten million people. At this point, our resources will crumble, and civil wars could be imminent. We keep building up as we look for other locations to settle. But is Mars our best bet? I've often wondered why we haven't paid more attention to our waters and learned to live, protected under the seas.

But what a beautiful place.

Even though our planet is dangerous, the torrential rain and the sun's energy put our rock into perspective. I've been lucky enough to see more of the world than most will be able to, and I tried to make each encounter a learning experience. There are so many places I haven't been to yet, and more that I will never see in this life, but these are locations that have astonished me over my life and created some memories that will last forever. I honestly believe that beauty is in the eye of the beholder, and it appears everywhere around us in many ways.

For thirteen years, I lived on Vancouver Island, on the west coast of Canada. The unique smells, the wildlife, the culture, and the history of the land and waters make this location tops on my list. But Canada is blessed with spectacular beauty. From the vast Rocky Mountains in Alberta and British Columbia to the majestic east coast, the country boasts a huge array of photogenic moments.

A Cognitive Project

Even the flat prairie lands of Canada, specifically in Saskatchewan, extract a different type of beauty. A serenity and genuine feeling of peace. There's something to long, flat distances that calm the soul and allow the mind to open and fully flourish. It brings safety and Zen.

I would have to admit that Spain's Southern coast was probably my favourite place outside of Canada. The warmth and culture there taught me at a young age that life was dissimilar around the world. People did things a different way, and it intrigued me greatly. In Europe, there are close seconds for beauty. The Bavarian region of Germany, and the fairytale presence of Switzerland, Austria and Lichtenstein will make you feel like you're inside of a storybook. And the people are friendly too.

If you're a fan of rich history, nothing compares to England, Germany, Italy, France or Northern Africa, where castles, dungeons, ancient coliseums, and the pyramids reside. Long, regal rivers and architecture from a time, long behind us. Of course, other places in the world are rich in history, but I can only comment on my personal experiences. We are so fortunate to share this place with the living animals and plants that flourish.

If I had to guess where beauty exists, I would think Australia and New Zealand are unique. Or a place close by like Fiji. We know some of the most exclusive animal species in the world come from these places. Places like Cambodia or Vietnam look lush and alive. The weather patterns there create beauty, and this is *not* a place of war.

Even the cold northern lands of Alaska offer stunning amounts of beauty, like whales to cascading glaciers, one can find absolute splendour worldwide. Even a damaged planet will heal, but I think we all worry about the human being's impact on the planet. Being the most intelligent species certainly doesn't stand well with us. The plastic and garbage we push into our waterways are disgusting. How can we consciously even do this to one another? We will continue to try and live our short lives in comfort and luxury. We seem to have trouble seeing how the future generations will cope, but we are selfish sometimes, only interested in our own immediate gains.

Maybe the Continent of Antarctica isn't the prettiest place on Earth, but it seems to be the most mysterious place on the planet. Most of us think of this place as a massive sheet of ice, and you're not wrong, but it's what's underneath that ice that has scientists scrambling to set up stations on the gigantic, barren piece of land.

There, some aquatic species exist that have yet to be discovered. Some of these species could have survived the ice ages and molten events, meaning these animals may have a lineage that stems back billions of years.

Some will even say that a secret alien base is located on Antarctica, or perhaps a human-made fortress made to establish communication with outer world's intelligence. I don't know about that, but anything is possible, I guess.

One thing is for sure. We are lucky. We are fortunate to have such a beautiful home, and I'm well aware that many share an atrocious life on this planet. It once again comes down to money and greed. The rich will flourish, and the poor will suffer. It's been an unfortunate trait for thousands of years, creating war and dire misfortune.

For those who are fortunate to have luxuries in their lives, take care of Earth. It remains our only option for a home, and we have nothing comparable right now. Do good and appreciate what you have. Love the ones you trust the most and always reach for goals to inspire you.

Each chapter in this book has to do with the way our brains accept information. We know we still have a lot to learn, but look at what we've already achieved. We don't all need to be innovators, but with the tremendous population spikes that we face, we owe it to our planet to work together for peace. It's something that has been lacking since day one of humanity, but just *imagine what could be accomplished if seven or eight billion people worked together to set a common goal.* Imagine a world without greed. Imagine a global push for peace and hope.

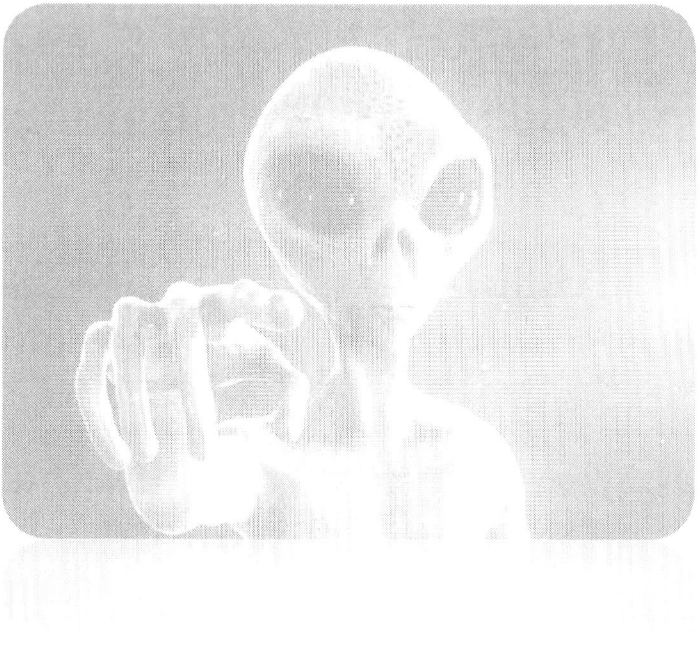

A Cognitive Project

Acknowledgments

I would like to thank my good friend of more than twenty-five long years, *Matthew Broughton*. He has supported my various opinions since day one, and we've shared some deep conversations over the years. Few can say they have a trusted friend they can rely upon through thick and thin over several years. I appreciate having someone solid in my life that understands who I am and challenges me to become a better individual.

And of course, thank you to my editor and wife, Sandra.

Research References

Google

The Bible

Wikipedia

Google Earth

YouTube Channels

Independent Foundations

The 9/11 Commission Report

The Warren Commission Report

Friends, Family, Teachers and Influencers

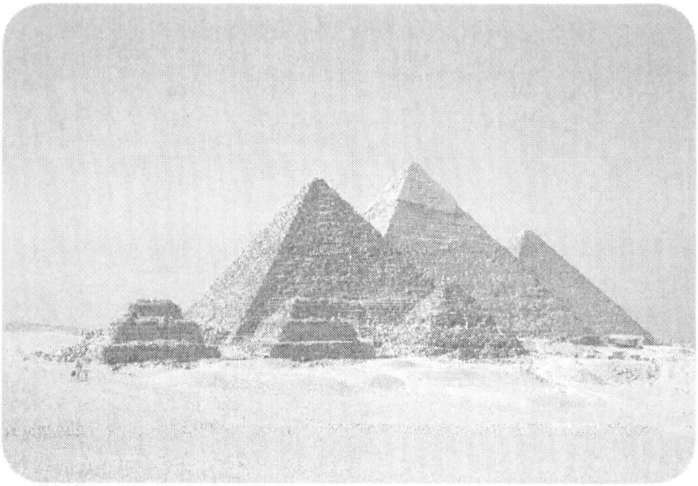

About the Author

Steven Blackwell is thrilled to offer his first non-fiction work since 232 Birch. In only seven years, Blackwell has managed to generate a total of six published works and has already started on the sequel to the volume you've just inspected, appropriately called *A Second Cognitive Project*.

Blackwell lives in Red Deer, Alberta, with his wife and two grown children, working full-time for a successful software corporation and writing whenever he has the chance. Expect more in the near future and fade away into the mysteries of the paranormal realm. It's an ambiguous realm that envelops each of us, begging for immediate enlightenment and intriguing us to understand.

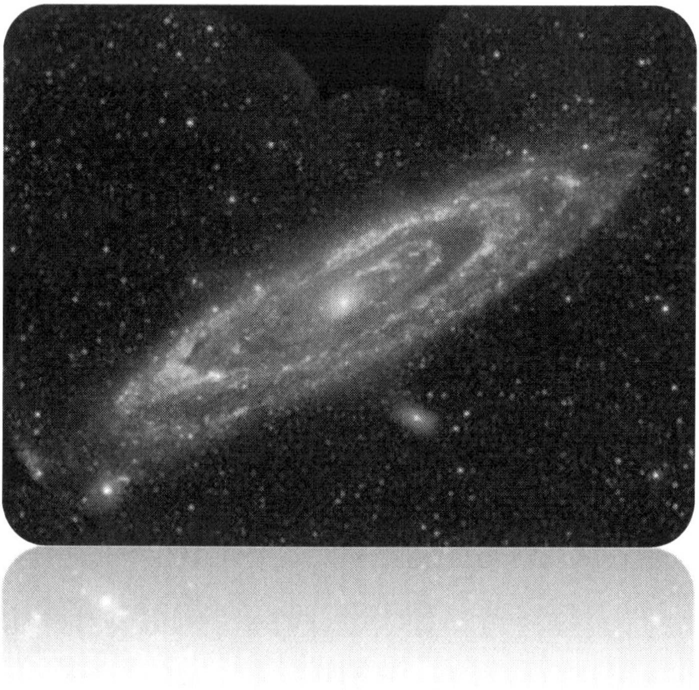

Keyword Glossary

Alien: VIII-IV, 10, 14-15, 19, 114, 119, 129, 155, 160, 171, 211

Animal: IV, 13, 16, 44-46, 94, 98-100, 165,191-195, 197-199, 209- 210

Assassination: III, X, 131-132, 136-137, 141-143, 146, 151-153

Atmosphere: 12, 113-114, 117,124, 183, 188-192, 194-195, 198-199, 203

Bible: I, 87-89,94,96-97,99-100, 102, 104, 185, 202, VIV

Book Depository: 133,136-137,139, 141, 146, 148-150, 152

Building: VIII, 2, 10-12, 19-33, 37, 40-43, 79-80, 113-114, 141, 148-149, 161, 187, 189, 208

Conspiracy: III-IV, VII, 24,31,45,117,125,131-132,134-135, 137-138, 141-144

Continent:126,183,188-190, 192, 194-197, 199-200, 204, 210

Christianity: IX, 85,89,91-92,101, 104, 106

Earth: II, X, XI, 12-13,17,35,42,56,83,85,97-98, 103, 109, 112-129, 131, 138, 162,164,169,171,183-201, 203-208, 210-211, XIV

Earthquake:158,197-198, 200, 205

Evidence: VI, 3-8, 14-16, 18-19,24-25,30-32, 34-35, 37, 42, 89, 100-101, 104,109, 117-118, 120, 131-134, 138, 140-143, 161, 173-174, 184,201-202

Galaxy: 111,115-116, 126-127

Game:45,54,57-59,86,186

Ghost: 2,6,10-11,19,83,104

God: I, II, IX, 61, 85-92,94,97,100-107, 185

Grassy Knoll: II, 131,134-135, 138-139, 141, 144, 148-151

Nine Eleven / 9-11: III, VIII, X, XIV, 21, 23, 25-26, 37-39, 42, 131, 155, 164-166, 169-170, 203, 205

Opinion: I, IV-V, VII-XI, 4, 6, 14, 27, 30-31, 35, 43, 89, 105-106, 109, 115-117, 119, 124, 132, 147-148, 152, 171, 181,183,203,207, XIV

Ocean / Sea: 1,15, 35, 42, 61-62, 64, 75-76, 78, 121, 124, 166, 171, 183, 186, 188-190, 191-192, 194-197, 199-200, 206-208

Oswald: III, X, 132-138, 142-147, 149-151, 153

Paranormal: VIII, 1-5, 8-10, 14, 16-19, 25, 89, XVI

People: II, IV, 2, 5, 7, 16, 18-19, 22-23, 25, 28, 33, 25-36, 39, 42-43, 57, 73, 80,85,88,90-93, 102-103, 105, 111, 124-125, 138-139, 143, 150, 152-153, 163,166,168-171, 183, 199, 202, 204, 207-209, 211

Planes / Airplanes / Aircraft: III, VIII, 13, 20, 23, 25-28, 30-32, 34, 37, 39, 41, 43

President: X, 38,131-143, 145-146, 148-150, 152-153

Pyramid: X, 154-167, 171, 203, 209

Quantum: X, 173-175, 179-180

Reality: X, 5-7, 10, 17, 26,97-98,103, 105, 116, 118, 172-175, 178, 180-181, 203

Religion: I, IX, 83-86, 88-92, 101, 104-106, 114, 202, 207

Science: X, 5-6, 26-27, 29, 33, 75, 98, 105, 155, 173-174, 181, 185

Solar System: 109-112, 116, 119, 123, 126-129, 185, 187

Space: IX, 1, 11, 13, 37, 57, 92, 107, 109-110, 112-113, 116-119, 121-122, 124-125, 160, 164, 166, 174, 185-188, 190, 197, 203

Spirit: VIII, XII, 1-4, 6-11, 19

Star: IX, 12, 93-96, 111-113, 117, 121-123, 126-127, 162, 183, 186

Sun: 12, 46, 84-85, 87, 92-96, 101, 103-104, 109-114, 116, 119, 122-123, 126-129, 163, 166, 183, 185-186, 190, 192, 198, 201, 208

Theory: II, VII, 31, 90, 92, 124-125,131, 140-141, 158,163,171-174, 179-181, 185

Universe: I, X, XII, 10-11, 83, 106-109, 112, 114-117, 119, 121-123, 125-126, 129, 173, 177-178, 180

World: II-V, X-XI, 10, 12-13, 18-25, 30-33, 38-39, 41-42, 61, 76, 79, 90, 94, 96, 99, 101, 106, 112, 114, 121, 132, 153, 155, 159. 164-165, 168-169, 172, 183, 194, 196, 198, 205-211

Made in the USA
Columbia, SC
08 June 2021